Memoirs & Critiques
of
Family & Church Dynamics

Pathway to Wholeness
By Jarvis "Jimmy" Ross

From Me

To You

The House I Lived in at Five Years Old, 1955

York Street, Camden, South Carolina

Memoirs & Critiques of Family & Church Dynamics (Pathway to Wholeness)

by Jarvis "Jimmy" Ross

Publication Information

Troutman, North Carolina

December 2025

Editor: Jarvis J. Ross @ JJPlanter.com

No part of this book may be reproduced or transmitted in any form or by any means, electronic or mechanical, including photocopying, recording, or by any information storage and retrieval system, without permission in writing from the publisher.

"Scripture quotations taken from the Amplified® Bible (AMPC),

Copyright © 1954, 1958, 1962, 1964, 1965, 1987 by The Lockman Foundation
Used by permission. www.Lockman.org"

About the Author and Work

Ross, Jarvis "Jimmy"

Memoirs & Critiques of Family & Church Dynamics (Pathway to Wholeness)

All events mentioned are true to the best of the author's memory, and the names of people and specific places have been omitted to protect their privacy rights.

ISBN: **978-1-7351195-7-1**

Cover design by Christina@diagonalleigh

Preface

In September 2025, I felt compelled to share testimonials about my family's history, heritage, and legacy. This decision was deeply personal and accompanied by the inclusion of meaningful photographs that captured the essence of our journey. Unexpectedly, it opened a door for an unknown family member, my brother's daughter, Shannon, and her sister, Tonya, to connect with me. Shannon was overwhelmed with tears, and so was I. The other good news was the input of current family members, who chimed in with positive enthusiasm.

In the past few years, I have been feeling a burden because of what I perceived as baggage that lingered, not just in my extended family, but within a segment of the collective community of what I refer to as Afrocentric Families. In my view, it created an atmosphere of negativity, impacting not merely our families but also those outside our circle who were unfamiliar with the full scope of our experiences.

Motivated by certain circumstances, I was moved to share truth from a higher perspective about our mutual family history and heritage and conclude with a positive legacy to help create a better understanding of what transpired in the past that affected the present.

Many in the younger generations, particularly Gen-Z, are somewhat disconnected from the history and heritage of the struggles of the past that contributed to a fragmented family history. Observing from a distance, they may underestimate the lasting impact that segregation and economic scarcity had on our communities. Despite these challenges, signs of hope are emerging. Awareness is growing, and new opportunities are unfolding for families to thrive spiritually, economically, and collectively. My spiritual sense and conviction is that God is moving with a distinct purpose to reconnect us to our history and heritage, not just from a natural lineage, but from a spiritual line of descent through Christ, Yeshua Hamashiach.

This book represents the story of our legacy: two hundred pages filled with thoughtful, inspired, real-life stories that reflect common human experiences. Each narrative is crafted with the intention of guiding readers toward higher truth and a path to exponential blessings.

As we explore the struggles and challenges associated with moving from brokenness to wholeness, it is important to note that our struggle is not against other people. As believers, we are clearly instructed not to engage in conflict with others simply for the sake of it. Paul, for example, advised his protégé Timothy in II Timothy 2:24-25 not to become embroiled in quarrels. Instead, we are called to "fight the good fight of faith" (I Timothy 6:12). That is the essence of the battles recounted in this book—winning the lost for Christ and uniting people of faith.

To illustrate the kind of struggles I have encountered, I want to share a practical spiritual experience from my ministry. In 2009, I was in the process of launching my second multiethnic church, this time within a Eurocentric denomination. **(See the Introduction for an explanation of the terms Eurocentric and Afrocentric.)** As with any church plant, securing funding was essential. During a meeting with a group of Eurocentric ministers, I was asked to present my concept for the new church. After my presentation, the ministers would vote to approve or deny the funding.

During the discussion, one minister asked whether the church plant would be based on a hip-hop typology, a question I found rather unusual. With some trepidation, I replied, "Of course not." Another minister immediately stood up and responded to the disparaging comment and called out the question as racist, which led to a back-and-forth debate among those present. The minister who first raised the question then made a motion not to fund the church plant.

Feeling discouraged, I sat down and quietly told the pastor who had recruited me, "I'm leaving." He urged me to stay, but I picked up my briefcase and headed to my car. As I was placing my briefcase in the trunk, I felt the unmistakable presence of the Lord come over me. I clearly heard a voice instruct me, "Go back in." Without hesitation, I obeyed, returned to the meeting, and took my seat.

By the time I rejoined, the debate was nearly over. As I sat, I sensed the Lord's presence move toward the minister who had made the motion. Unexpectedly, he stood up and said he would rescind his motion not to fund and instead moved to approve funding. Moments like these have shaped my journey—they represent the type of spiritual battles I have faced for most of my life and form the central theme of this book.

Introduction

What follows is a reflection on a common journey: the transformation from brokenness to wholeness.

Through a combination of memoirs and critiques, this book explores the dynamic changes in family and church life that profoundly affect individuals and their loved ones. These stories, drawn from real-life adventures, are both thrilling and heart-wrenching. They underscore the significance of testimonies in overcoming adversity and discovering renewal in faith.

These memoirs chart both personal and collective transformation through sequentially numbered chapters taken from real-life experiences that overlap and recap events. The goal is to narrate and inspire readers from the first person—individuals and families alike—to confront and release toxic thoughts, emotional burdens, and lingering baggage from the past. Central to this process is an appreciation of family history, heritage, and legacy, which serve as anchors and sources of strength on the path to healing.

This journey unfolds in three essential stages, each examined through shared testimonies and spiritual critiques:

> **Stage 1: Journey through Familial Brokenness.** The initial stage delves into the challenges and fractures within families, illuminating the impact these experiences have on personal growth and relationships.
>
> **Stage 2: Confronting & Growing through Church Conflicts.** Next, the narrative addresses the trials faced within church communities, highlighting how individuals

confront conflict and develop spiritually through these struggles.

Stage 3: Wounded Healers in Action—Brokenness Made Whole. Finally, the stories reveal how those who have experienced brokenness become agents of healing, demonstrating the process of being made whole through faith and service.

Pathway to Higher Truth centers on the cleansing of the soul. It emphasizes the importance of healing and spiritual growth, presenting a blueprint for uniting people of faith. The narrative extends beyond healing to lay the foundation for lasting unity through **Christ**, the **Foundation**, and laying the **Building Stones**: *Disciplined Correction, Mutual Accountability, Cross Reconciliation*, and *Holistic Restoration*. These building stones ensure ongoing support and connection among all family members, culminating in **faith-driven steps** toward wholeness and a personal testimony of physical healing from cancer from Yours Truly. **Connected, they guide relationships in the right direction by word and deed.**

Ultimately, this story explores the nature of God's everlasting Kingdom on Earth, the journey toward eternal bliss, and perspectives on the afterlife. It affirms that God's Kingdom stands as the ultimate reality, both in this life and for all eternity.

Changing the Narrative & the Conversation

The final section, Pathway to Higher Truth, underscores the critical role of clear thinking in nurturing unfiltered faith that cleanses the soul of obstacles and prepares the heart for deeper understanding. This section delves into practical approaches for grasping higher biblical truths, highlighting the significance of each individual's personal journey of faith and their pursuit of the gift of eternal life as presented in Scripture.

This section also examines the nature of God's Kingdom, offering insight into differing religious perspectives on the afterlife. It addresses the ongoing process of spiritual and holistic healing, emphasizing the importance of **"God-Talk"**—the practice of spiritual analysis woven into everyday conversations—as a means to achieve this transformation.

Throughout this work, specific terminology has been carefully chosen to reflect cultural descent rather than traditional racial classifications. Terms such as **"Eurocentric"** and **"Afrocentric"** are intentionally used to denote ethnic cultural descent, in harmony with scriptural references to nations—translated as **"ethnos"** or **ethnic**—instead of race.

The deliberate selection of "Eurocentric" and "Afrocentric" serves a significant purpose. By drawing attention to divisions rooted in cultural perspectives rather than in individuals themselves, these terms encourage a more thoughtful examination of history, heritage, and legacy. This shift in focus acknowledges that cultural divisions and animosities are complex, having origins that cannot be attributed to a single group or direction. Such divisions are prevalent across various contexts and must be recognized and confronted to achieve true reconciliation.

Grasping the nuances of these terms is essential for meaningful engagement with the broader discussion presented in this work. Acknowledging and healing persistent cultural divisions—which are deeply embedded within historical and cultural contexts and can foster bigotry—is imperative. Readers who wish to explore these challenges and potential paths to resolution are encouraged to consult the section titled **"Why Unifying Afrocentric People is Complicated but Possible!"**

While the discussion weighs the experiences of different ethnicities and cultures, the central focus remains on unifying all people of faith. The Book of Ephesians offers guidance for this pursuit. In **Ephesians 4:1-5**, the Apostle Paul writes:

I therefore, the prisoner for the Lord, appeal to and beg you to walk (lead a life) worthy of the [divine] calling to which you have been called [with behavior that is a credit to the summons to God's service, Living as becomes you] with complete lowliness of mind (humility) and meekness (unselfishness, gentleness, mildness), with patience, bearing with one another and making allowances because you love one another.

Be eager and strive earnestly to guard and keep the harmony and oneness of [and produced by] the Spirit in the binding power of peace.

[There is] one body and one Spirit—just as there is also one hope [that belongs] to the calling you received—

[There is] one Lord, one faith, one baptism,

One God and Father of [us] all, Who is above all [Sovereign over all], pervading all and [living] in [us] all.

This passage provides the prescription for unity among people of faith: humility, gentleness, patience, and a commitment to love, peace, and oneness. By embracing these virtues, believers can overcome divisions and strive toward true reconciliation and holistic healing.

In The End

As we reach the final page of this book, a powerful and transformative concept is revealed regarding the battle against spiritual evil. This kingdom principle for "Combating Spiritual Evil: Overcoming Oppression Through Spiritual Warfare" stands out for its practical application and common-sense approach.

Unlike traditional methods that may involve protesting, marching, or interfering with law enforcement, this concept encourages a different route. It proposes that victory over spiritual oppression can be achieved without external actions that disrupt or confront authorities directly.

This approach is a true eye-opener, offering readers a practical and effective way to address spiritual challenges. The principle presented here provides clarity and insight, making it both accessible and sensible for those seeking to overcome spiritual evil through means rooted in spiritual warfare.

Stage I: Journey through Familial Brokenness

I. Embracing Life's Transitions: A Journey of Faith and Renewal

Wholeness is soundness of mind, body, soul, and spirit, and a well-rounded life. Here, we examine and explore the first stage to wholeness, leading up to Christ and the gift of salvation.

Life, in all its forms—plants, animals, and humans—progresses through a series of developmental stages. While plants and animals transition instinctively through evolutionary processes, humans experience growth in a more gradual, chronological manner, moving from infancy through adulthood to old age. The crucial period between infancy and old age is when we form our adult identity. If we fail to establish our sense of self at any stage, immaturity is carried forward, affecting our perspective and attitude toward life, ourselves, and others. Comments about change—whether positive or negative—reflect this ongoing process. In the following sections, we will focus on positive changes, examining life's dynamics objectively.

Our spiritual and familial responsibilities call us to adapt, adjust, and accept life's changes. Instead of judging others based on earlier stages of development, we should encourage and uplift one another, using edifying words that motivate growth. This approach emphasizes the positive and discards the negative. Ultimately, we recognize that transformation in others is beyond our control; only God can bring about true change. Our goal is to appreciate differences through the lens of divine design, setting the stage for deeper exploration.

Before sharing my personal testimony, it is important to honor the experiences of those who came before us. Their unwavering faith through uncertainty and hardship serves as a source of inspiration and hope, reminding us that our journey is not solitary. My parents, separated for much of my life, demonstrated courage in adversity, which inspired me despite the lack of nurturing and parenting.

Listening to one another's testimonies helps us understand individual histories, fostering empathy and connection regardless of past experiences. Each act of trust and perseverance in the past contributes to a legacy of faith that continues to encourage us today.

Faith's journey often requires releasing burdens from our past. Drawing inspiration from **Hebrews 12:1**, I have witnessed this scriptural principle at work in my own life as a testament to God's faithfulness.

Hebrews 12:1 urges believers to examine the weights they carry: ***"Therefore then, since we are surrounded by so great a cloud of witnesses [who have borne testimony to the Truth], let us strip off and throw aside every encumbrance (unnecessary weight) and that sin which so readily (deftly and cleverly) clings to and entangles us, and let us run with patient endurance and steady and active persistence the appointed course of the race that is set before us."*** This reference to Hebrews chapter eleven recalls the "Heroes and Heroines" of faith—those who achieved greatness through trust in God without seeing the fulfillment of Messianic promises. Their example encourages us to persevere, knowing that we have witnessed the fulfillment they anticipated.

Laying Aside Burdens and Embracing Our New Identity

The passage, *"let us strip off and throw aside every encumbrance (unnecessary weight) and that sin which so readily (deftly and cleverly) clings to and entangles us"* urges believers to release the burdens that impede spiritual growth. These burdens frequently arise from our past and are connected to our former, unregenerate selves. However, as followers of Christ, we are called to depend on our renewed identity and nature. By letting go of these weights, we can walk in true freedom.

The Scripture encourages us to *"and let us run with patient endurance and steady and active persistence the appointed course of the race that is set before us."* Here, patience signifies endurance, likening our faith journey to a marathon rather than a sprint. This race is not about competing with others or measuring ourselves against their achievements. Instead, it is a personal journey, focused solely on Christ, who serves as our life coach. Our goal is to finish the course that fulfills our individual mission and calling.

Within the Body of Christ, believers share a common mission: to continue witnessing for Christ until we are called home. The Apostle Paul recounts this mission in **Philippians 3:7-14**, which culminates in the promise of immortal, glorified bodies. Until that time comes, our primary calling is to share our faith, beginning with those closest to us, as ministry starts at home **(Acts 1:8)**.

Endurance is vital to our spiritual journey, especially when facing difficulties. Our strength to persevere is found by fixing our eyes on Jesus, who is the ultimate example of faith and endurance. **Hebrews 12:2-3** emphasizes this focus: ***"Looking away [from all that will distract] to Jesus, Who is the Leader and the Source of our faith [giving the first incentive for our belief] and is also its Finisher [bringing it to maturity and perfection]. He, for the joy [of obtaining the prize] that was set before Him, endured the cross, despising and ignoring the shame, and is now seated at the right hand of the throne of God.***

Just think of Him Who endured from sinners such grievous opposition and bitter hostility against Himself [reckon up and consider it all in comparison with your trials], so that you may not grow weary or exhausted, losing heart and relaxing and fainting in your minds."

This reminder encourages believers to remain steadfast, knowing that the Lord goes before us and lightens our load.

Throughout my life, I have witnessed the renewal that comes from the Lord, especially in the realm of spiritual growth as described in **Psalm 103:5**. This renewal has had a profound effect on my mental clarity, emotional balance, and physical health, even at the age of 75. The guilt and burdens from my past, which once weighed me down and left me unmotivated, have been lifted. This release is in accordance with the promise found in **Hebrews 12:1-3**.

—*What We Believe Is Significant*—

I do not subscribe to the belief often referred to as the **"curse of the generations,"** which is sometimes taught based on interpretations of Old Testament passages such as **Exodus 20:5**. This perspective suggests that family heritage can be the reason for missing blessings or the need for deliverance, and can be used to explain the absence of promised health, wealth, and prosperity. However, the New Testament, and the Gospel in particular, refute this claim under the New Covenant Provisions.

Such beliefs may lead individuals to blame their family background for current hardships and create distance from loved ones. Instead, Scripture teaches that through Christ, we are redeemed from the **"curse of the law"** and inherit the **"blessings of Abraham" (Galatians 3:13)**, which include all the promises of the Covenant.

In my relationships, I strive to walk in the freedom that comes through Christ, the bridge between life and relationships, by holding no animosity toward anyone. As **Romans 14:7-8** states, *"None of us lives to himself [but to the Lord], and none of us dies to himself [but to the Lord, for] If we live, we live to the Lord, and if we die, we die to the Lord. So then, whether we live or we die, we belong to the Lord."*

While it is possible to carry burdens passed down from previous generations, these do not have to define who we are today. Through repentance, confession, and renunciation, we can release these burdens. This act of surrender brings true freedom, enabling us to move forward unencumbered by the past.

With a clear conscience, free from guilt, remorse, and regret, I have chosen to forgive both those I have wronged and those who have wronged me. This is because God's work in me is ongoing—and He is not finished with you, either.

The reason I can move forward with a clear heart is simple: God's work in my life is not yet complete. Just as He continues to shape and mold me, He is also at work in your life. We are both in the process of becoming who we are meant to be, and neither of our journeys is finished.

Because of this, I am determined to finish the race—the mission that God has set before me, engaging my calling and purpose.

II. Knowing your Heritage and Legacy

Heritage represents the history and legacy passed down through our families. While many individuals, especially minorities, have faced misfortune and disenfranchisement and therefore may inherit little or nothing materially from their ancestors, heritage encompasses much more than material possessions. The most meaningful aspect of heritage is the **influence** of **character**, **values**, and **cherished memories** that are transmitted from one generation to the next, shaping the direction of our lives and our future. But it is important to remember that the memories that we carry must be weighed in the balance of God's Word to accentuate the positive and eliminate the negative that falls in the category of fallen human nature. Believers in Christ are not fallen but have been raised to sit in heavenly places in Christ. **Ephesians 2:5-6,** *"Even when we were dead (slain) by [our own] shortcomings and trespasses, He made us alive together in fellowship and in union with Christ; [He gave us the very life of Christ Himself, the same new life with which He quickened Him, for] it is by grace (His favor and mercy which you did not deserve) that you are saved (delivered from judgment and made partakers of Christ's salvation). And He raised us up together with Him and made us sit down together [giving us joint seating with Him] in the heavenly sphere [by virtue of our being] in Christ Jesus (the Messiah, the Anointed One)."*

Our heritage is not confined solely to our natural family lineage and is a matter of faith. For those who are in Christ and redeemed by His sacrifice, the concept of **bloodline** expands and extends beyond familial ties to include the family of God. **Acts 17:26a,** *"And He made from one [common origin, one source, one blood] all nations of men to settle on the face of the earth, having definitely determined [their] allotted periods of time and the fixed boundaries of their habitation (their settlements, lands, and abodes)."* This spiritual heritage is significant because it elevates our sense of **self-worth** in the Lord. In Christ, we are considered royalty, as children of the King.

Even biblical figures experienced challenges related to family and heritage. For example, David, who felt abandoned by his family while he was a fugitive, reminded us of the enduring legacy and heritage we have in the Lord. As stated in **Psalms 27:10**: *"Although my father and my mother have forsaken me, yet the Lord will take me up [adopt me as His child]."* During my adolescent and young adult years, I felt left alone by my parents, but the Lord stood in the gap and discipleship provided parenting by a higher authority. I was raised in the Lord.

From a biological perspective, heritage refers to heredity—the passing down of physical characteristics from parents to their offspring. This process contributes to our sense of identity and belonging. The shared history we possess with our ancestors helps create a common sense of purpose among us.

Family History & Testimonies

To illustrate the importance of shared purpose in the Lord, I will begin sharing my family history through personal testimonies. These stories highlight how our common purpose is shaped by both our family legacy and our spiritual heritage.

History and heritage occur by ebbs and flows, by coming and going, declining and inclining—it vacillates back and forth.

As we consider the historical testimonies concerning family, it is essential to understand that history does not occur in isolation, like a vacuum. Rather than unfolding in a linear sequence, both history and Scripture present events that overlap and revisit previous moments, requiring us to connect chronological points and recognize their interwoven patterns. This complexity means that consequences and events rarely follow a straightforward path.

Winston Churchill, in his 1948 speech, famously warned, "Those who fail to learn from history are doomed to repeat it." While this is a powerful admonition, it is important to clarify that, from a scientific and genetic standpoint, history does not literally repeat itself. True repetition would imply an impossible reversal of time and the Earth's rotation. Still, the patterns within history tend to resurface, especially when unresolved issues from the past continue to affect the present. This is particularly true for family problems that remain unaddressed and linger across generations.

Turning to the present, it is necessary to acknowledge the persistent residue and legacy of slavery and segregation. These historical circumstances contributed to, but did not single-handedly cause, divisions among people of color today. Regardless of the past, one's responsibility in the present is to pursue a better life without excusing our problems from the past. Of particular importance is the impact of segregation, which forced those emancipated from slavery to reside in the ghettos of America through Jim Crow laws. The crowded conditions and limited resources in these neighborhoods led to increased crime, violence, and immorality as residents competed for scarce resources.

As low-income Afrocentric people moved into these areas that were occupied by Eurocentric residents, the Eurocentric residents often relocated, establishing suburban communities by opposing desegregation efforts. This movement led to the development of a "self-hate psychology" among some Afrocentric people, who followed the path to suburbia, assimilated into the norms of their Eurocentric counterparts, and viewed their origins with disdain and blame. Such blame was encapsulated in the phrase, "pull yourself up by your own bootstraps," even though many lacked the means to do so. Over time, the history of these struggles has become obscured by newer generations of Afrocentric people, who focus on achievement and affluence, often through material possessions. This shift has resulted in the misperception that the hardships faced by Afrocentric people were self-inflicted, which perpetuates further arguments and division.

An illustrative analogy can be found in the 1994 animated film "The Lion King," which explores themes of heritage, history, and legacy. In the story, Simba's father, Mufasa, is killed by his brother, Scar, who manipulates Simba into believing he is responsible for the tragedy. Simba flees into exile, eventually collapsing in the desert, where he is rescued and nurtured by Timon and Pumbaa, a meerkat and warthog duo. Years later, Simba's future Queen, Nala, locates him and, with the help of Rafiki, the seer, encourages him to return to the Pride Lands and reclaim his rightful place as king.

A pivotal moment occurs when Simba and his friends express the philosophy "hakuna matata"—meaning "it doesn't matter, it's in the past." Rafiki strikes Simba with his staff, and when Simba protests, "Ow! Jeez! What was that for?" Rafiki responds, "It doesn't matter. It's in the past." This scene underscores the idea that unresolved and unreconciled issues from divided relationships, if ignored, can continue to cause pain. Simba's return and reclamation of his throne symbolize the necessity for us to reclaim our God-given legacy and heritage as children of the King, our Lord, remaining connected to our natural bloodline, with Christ serving as the bridge in relationships.

This idea becomes particularly relevant when examining family heritage. Although I have already addressed and refuted the misunderstanding or misinterpretation of Scripture regarding the so-called "curse of the generations," it remains true that we can inherit and pass on burdens from our past. These burdens, however, are not unbreakable. In the spiritual context, they are judicially annulled in God's courtroom when we come to Christ. What remains is the process of

"breaking the yoke"—removing the oppressive influences handed down through generations.

In **Isaiah 10**, the prophet Isaiah predicts the impending oppressive dominion of the Assyrian government in exile and points out that the judgment can be broken if Israel returns to the Promise of God's Covenant. The source of the **pressure** and **stress** for the people of God came from a foreign oppressive government. **Be careful of the source of information about your family heritage, especially if it's bad news. It will cause stress and pressure that exacerbates the problem to a greater degree.** It's like the old school game "**pass it on**." Twenty people gathered in a circle received some information and were told to pass it on to the next person. By the time it gets to the last person, it can become a completely different story. That's the way gossip and rumors work. That includes news that comes from various media sources, as well as family and friends. In that light, burdens and baggage from the past can be averted if we heed God's Word instead of allowing the sources mentioned to feed our minds with thoughts that distract from God's Word.

The prophet Isaiah, in **Isaiah 10**, speaks of this promise of liberation from unjust burdens. **Isaiah 10:27** declares, *"And it shall be in that day that the burden of [the Assyrian] shall depart from your shoulders, and his yoke from your neck. The yoke shall be destroyed because of fatness [which prevents it from going around your neck]."* This passage assures believers that, through the anointing, oppressive legacies are destroyed, and the burdens are lifted. When we are in Christ, we receive a

new nature, the **Spirit of God,** through the **New Covenant Promise** that grants us a new heritage by connecting us to the promises of Abraham.

It is achieved through **confession** that identifies our error of judgment; **repentance**, **sorrow**, recognizing that we have wrongly judged others; and **renouncing** the judgment by disowning it. **This simple process evokes toxic feelings.** This is how we let go of the burdens of the past. **Hebrews 12:1** urges us to lay aside every weight and sin that so easily entangles us, running with perseverance the race set before us.

When we are in Christ, we have divine assurance of freedom in Christ. The **New Covenant Promise** establishes that believers are connected to the promises given to Abraham, granting us a renewed heritage. As **Galatians 3:6-9** explains:

- Even as Abraham *"Thus Abraham believed in and adhered to and trusted in and relied on God, and it was reckoned and placed to his account and credited as righteousness (as conformity to the divine will in purpose, thought, and action")*

- Therefore, those who are of faith are considered the children of Abraham.

- The Scripture foresaw that God would justify the Gentiles by faith and proclaimed the Gospel beforehand to Abraham, saying, *"in you shall all the nations [of the earth] be blessed"*

- Thus, those who are of faith are blessed alongside faithful Abraham.

Through faith in Christ, believers not only break free from the inherited burdens of the past but also step into the blessings promised to Abraham, forging a new spiritual heritage. Although one can be on the wrong side of history in their alternate reality, it cannot prevent the right side of history of God's purpose and plan from being fulfilled. **Instead of believing your family is cursed, know that you are blessed in Christ.**

III. My Family Testimony

Here, I will transition from my father's and mother's testimony, then to my older brothers, and to my own personal testimony.

Despite growing up in a segregated society with limited resources, both my parents managed to build respectable lives for themselves.

My Father's Journey

My Daddy, although he did not receive a formal education, became a well-known, respected, and honored maintenance man and custodian for the Macy's franchise. His achievements, though sometimes met with laughter or judgment, reflect resilience and dignity. Although I didn't grow up with my father in the home, I spent five years living with him during my adolescence, gaining a firsthand understanding of his character and work ethic.

Daddy was about 5'9" tall, thin, big-boned, and light-skinned. According to Momma, his great-grandfather was a six-foot-five Scottish Presbyterian preacher, which may explain both my height and my calling to preach, and the years I spent in the Presbyterian Church.

Daddy was a praying deacon in the Baptist Church during my childhood and was influenced by my older brother to move from Camden, SC, to Brooklyn, NY, for a better factory job. In Camden, he worked on the city roads, and in 1955, he relocated with Momma and four younger siblings to Brooklyn. However, the job did not work out, and he eventually disappeared from the home. My siblings and I saw him only occasionally as we sought his help, which was seldom found.

Momma and Daddy had twelve children, but three died as infants—Charles, Willie, and Barbara Jean—due to a lack of proper healthcare in a segregated society. As an adult, I believed Daddy left because he was ashamed of not being able to provide for his family. I also surmised that he severed ties with the family to put the pain of his past disappointments of failed responsibilities out of mind. But history has a way of catching up to us, and I believe that his severed past caught up to him in his senior years just before death.

The statement doesn't carry negative connotations. Instead, it is a fact of life that sooner or later we must face the good, bad, and ugly of our past. I see the senior years as a catch basin where memories of the past play back with either fondness or regret, and efforts to recapture missed opportunities that lead to a midlife crisis. Although I never saw my dad with another woman, just before he passed away, a younger woman lived with him and swindled him out of what resources he had and his insurance beneficiary claim before he passed.

In 2009, therapeutic counseling helped me process what I perceived as abandonment by my father, leading to emotional healing and the release of suppressed anger toward Daddy that left a "father wound."

From an early age, I suppressed feelings that my daddy didn't want me. Those feelings resurfaced again when I was nineteen, after my father put me out of the house. At that point, I recalled my father's words when he became inebriated and put two and two together. He would utter "no good" about me and my brothers. My father was a truly good man who felt compelled to care for his troubled sons, so I could at least empathize with him because our behavior was bad. I then discovered that I was more hurt and broken than angry. My healing involved releasing the anger and restoring the years that I lost from abandonment.

In **Joel 2:25-26**, the prophet Joel proclaims prophetically to the People of God that if they trust him in the midst of their pain, they will be restored. When the Lord "saves" us, He restores the years that we lost. ***"And I will restore or replace for you the years that the locust has eaten—the hopping locust, the stripping locust, and the crawling locust, My great army which I sent among you. And you shall eat in plenty and be satisfied and praise the name of the Lord, your God, Who has dealt wondrously with you. And My people shall never be put to shame."***

Today, I have prospered without animosity towards my dad and live in comfort and peace, content with enough to meet our family's needs and enjoy the benefits of life.

Throughout her life, Momma rarely spoke negatively about him, which reinforced the abandonment because I needed to know the truth.

They attempted reconciliation in 1964, and my younger siblings and I lived together as a family for only one year. They separated again in 1965 but never divorced. From 1964 to 1969, my brothers, Johnny and LaForn, and I lived with Daddy, while my mother moved on with my older sister, Elizabeth, in their own place, and my sister Vernell returned to Brooklyn.

During those years, I saw Daddy as a hardworking, quiet, and reserved man who took care of me, cooked for me, bought my clothes, gave me money, and provided my first 10-speed bicycle. He appeared lonely and would drink himself to sleep after work. I think because of the absence of his daughters in his life, he cared deeply for my wife, treating her as his own daughter.

In 1989, while I was pastoring in a city in Tennessee, Daddy called and asked me to come get him. Shortly after, he was hospitalized, and my wife and I traveled to Schenectady to visit him. When he saw me, he called out my nickname, "JIMMY," after his brother Jim. We spent hours together, sharing stories and praying for his salvation. He passed away the next day. We brought his body back to Camden and buried him in Bishopville, SC. Today, I have only fond memories of Daddy and take comfort in the belief that, according to his faith, he is now home with the Lord.

My Mother's Journey

My Momma was a petite, shapely, barely five feet, very dark-skinned woman who proudly celebrated her blackness and carried indigenous Indian heritage. Her love for people inspired me to appreciate diversity. She devoted herself to the Lord, praying fervently for her family each day and maintaining a spotless home as a perfectionist.

Momma worked tirelessly, picking cotton, cleaning houses, and caring for children as a nanny. I remember, at five years old in Camden, SC, riding in a canvas truck with Momma and my youngest siblings to the cotton fields. She would shield us from the sun with a sheet and haul huge bales of cotton to support the family. Momma was known for her friendliness and ability to connect with others, traits she passed on to me. She was also a faith healer and midwife, skills learned from her mother, Charlotte Hubbard.

Despite bearing twelve children, Momma remained physically, mentally, and emotionally strong. There was a seven-year gap between the births of her older and younger children. Three older siblings died in infancy from untreated sickness, and my oldest brother, Herbert Ross Junior, was tragically killed as a young adult. As the youngest, I never really knew my older siblings, who had moved on by the time I reached my teenage years.

Momma maintained her dignity in the face of modest circumstances, low income, and welfare assistance after Daddy left. She was steadfast and never allowed anyone or anything to diminish her self-worth. Despite a proper education, she earned her GED in her later years and became a well-known, well-respected, and honored Geriatric Nursing Assistant (CNA).

After Daddy left, she cared for me throughout my childhood and early adolescence. Even when Daddy forced me out of his place due to his perception of my lack of ambition, she always left the door open and the light on for me. My truth is, I felt held back and oppressed in a de facto segregated society, so I didn't know the course I should take to better my life because some opportunities were not available to me. I was a late bloomer, and my progress was slow, but I was determined to better my life.

Like an Eaglet leaving the nest of the Mother Eagle, I was determined to build my own nest and raise a close-knit family, not splintered by circumstances. Later, I learned that human fate is one thing and divine destiny is another. When I came to Christ, the Lord opened doors of opportunity for me that I didn't know existed.

IV. My Brothers: LaForn and Johnny

LaForn: A Story of Struggle and Strength

LaForn, my brother, eventually returned to Brooklyn, leaving me in the care of our father. Looking back as an adult, I believe that the sense of abandonment LaForn experienced had a severely damaging effect on him, ultimately contributing to his battle with mental illness later in life. His struggles were not solely the result of abandonment; his physical health also played a significant role. He suffered from untreated rheumatic fever, which led to inflammation and swelling in his ankles and caused him to walk with a limp, often appearing as though he was crippled. Years later, while high on drugs, he was hit by a cab and thrown ten feet, which shattered his bones in his right leg that had to be amputated. From my perspective, these health challenges and circumstances made him feel incomplete and incompetent. In response, he sometimes displayed violent outbursts, which I believe were manifestations of a deep-seated father wound.

Despite these difficulties, our family never placed blame for LaForn's illness on our father, and I believe this is as it should be. Instead, I feel that with proper medical attention from an early age, his condition could have improved.

Later in life, LaForn was diagnosed with Intermittent Explosive Disorder (IED). He was institutionalized as an adult after a drug-induced suicide attempt. Tragically, LaForn passed away in his mid-fifties and was isolated from his family.

Physically, LaForn stood out as the darkest-skinned member of our family and was tall at 6'1". He was handsome and known for being a womanizer. Despite the challenges he faced, LaForn left me with a positive legacy. He taught me valuable skills like riding a bike, playing handball, and basketball. Most importantly, he served as my protector, watching over me as his youngest brother on the streets of Brooklyn.

Johnny: Music, Mentorship, and Hardship

Johnny, the second-oldest brother, was two years older than LaForn, who in turn was two years older than me. Johnny was shorter, standing about 5'6", with brown skin and curly hair. He was also handsome and possessed a remarkable singing voice, described as similar to a nightingale.

When I was thirteen, my brothers and I formed a singing group called the Socialistic Lads. We sang doo-wop songs on the streets of Brooklyn, often while sharing wine. Johnny was the lead singer, LaForn sang baritone, I sang tenor, and an older friend provided the bass.

Johnny also played a significant role as my mentor from a young age, although some of his guidance led me astray. He taught me how to "hustle" for nickels and dimes on Broadway in Brooklyn and how to skip school. Despite the trouble these lessons sometimes brought, I loved Johnny deeply for his role as my mentor.

Johnny's relationship with our father was fraught with hostility, which I believe contributed to difficulties in his life. When our parents separated again in 1965, Johnny joined the Navy. After about two years, he returned home changed. Using the language of the time, he became a "wine-o," and his drinking worsened as the years passed. Johnny's life became marked by homelessness, public intoxication, and frequent jail stays for disturbing the peace. He lived with various people who often took advantage of his disability check, and, sadly, he died in his fifties, living in the attic of those who had taken him in.

As sad as these stories may sound, they are not disparaging or discouraging. Instead, it speaks of when examining the history of what has divided us, our eyes will tear up because of the pain of the past, which is why most don't want to talk about it. But we can't fix what's broken without identifying how it was broken. There is a bright side to every story, likened unto a bright light shining into darkness that overrides the bad with the good of God's purpose (Romans 8:28; Romans 5:20).

Detoxing from the Negative Past

The journey to spiritual healing begins with the process of detoxifying our inner selves. This path requires us to confront painful memories and experiences from our past, even though they may be uncomfortable or distressing. True healing is not possible without facing and working through these pains.

Discipleship, at its core, involves **"bearing our cross."** This phrase signifies the need to mortify our selfish tendencies and embark on a process of cleansing ourselves from negative emotions that originate from our fallen nature. A good natural analogy is that of a pearl. When a mere grain of sand finds its way into the hard outer shell of a pearl, it produces a substance called **"mother-of-pearl,"** or nacre. In the effort of the oyster to get rid of the irritant, the nacre becomes a pearl. Through the irritation of pain, in Christ, we become valuable like a pearl that is priceless in the eyes of others.

In contemporary terms, it means detoxing feelings such as **anger, bitterness, hate, resentment, envy, jealousy, strife, gossip, slander,** and character assassination—emotions and behaviors that hinder our relationships and spiritual growth.

While it is easy to focus on the negatives within ourselves and others, it is important to highlight the positives. There is more good in each person than bad. Christ's teachings emphasize the infinite value of every soul, declaring that each individual is worth more than the whole world **(Mark 8:36)**. Although Christ confronted the Pharisees with words that compared them to corrupt hypocrites, He never degraded humanity. He encouraged His followers to affirm the worth of every person.

However, human nature can be corrupted through exposure to toxic people and environments. We are born into this world with free will, and we can choose to follow the path of moral decline, and corruption can be nurtured in us. **Romans 12:1-3** speaks of the need for spiritual cleansing to overcome this corruption, suggesting that anyone can change through positive affirmation and renewal of the mind.

Detoxing, in this biblical context, serves to clarify our vision and help us find direction. By cleansing ourselves of harmful attitudes and impulses, we remove barriers that impede healthy relationships and spiritual growth.

The Bible further instructs us to lay aside all **malice**, **deceit**, **hypocrisy**, and **evil speaking (I Peter 2:1)**. Christ taught His disciples never to call another person worthless **(Matthew 5:22)**, urging us instead to recognize and affirm the inherent value in everyone.

Reflections on those Formative Years

Life in Brooklyn during the 1950s and 1960s was challenging due to gang violence and de facto segregation, with ethnic groups largely confined to their own neighborhoods. Going into a neighborhood where you didn't live was dangerous because of your ethnic and racial differences and neighborhood gangs. Momma did her best to protect us from the streets by providing food, clothing, and shelter, but her hands were tied when it came to our activities in school and on the streets. But it was different with my sister. She overprotected her from teen pregnancy, which created a taboo, and my sister became pregnant when she was in her late teens by a gang banger. Taboos become enticing when nature's impulses desire what's behind the taboo. An example is the tree of the Knowledge of Good and Evil. But we were allowed to roam the streets because her philosophy was, **"Boys will be boys."** This led us into trouble as we navigated the tough streets of Brooklyn due to a lack of parental guidance. My mother, as a single female head of the household, in some ways felt helpless to rescue her sons from the streets. Consequently, we had no boundaries to our behavior, and we began smoking, drinking, and carousing at an early age. (My mother's experience does not apply to all single female heads of household. Some single women have raised their children by themselves on very little, but different circumstances should be weighed.)

Although deeply spiritual, Momma rarely attended church but was dedicated to volunteering with the **Salvation Army** for 25 to 30 years. She faced her problems with faith and prayer. In her later years, diabetes claimed her life, and my wife and I visited her in the hospital during her final days. With a smile and sadness in her eyes (She always had sad eyes.), she told me, **"I prayed for two of my sons to become preachers, Curtis, and you, and my prayer has been answered. Do good..."** Inspired by her words, I excelled for over forty years, achieving a six-digit salary, reaching hundreds with the gospel, and always remembering my origins. We funeralized Momma and laid her to rest beside Daddy in **Bishopville**, **SC**.

V. My "Personal" Testimony

Searching for Meaning Amidst a Party Lifestyle

When my father put me out of his house in 1969, for several years, my girlfriend and I moved from one job and apartment to another, living a lifestyle centered around partying and carousing. During this period, I struggled with depression and felt a persistent sense that God was pressing upon me to change my life. This internal struggle came to a head during a party we hosted to welcome her brother home from prison. That night, under the influence of alcohol and marijuana, I got into a heated argument with two men who insisted that Allah was the path to God. Their claims clashed with what my mother had always witnessed in me about Christ, and I became both angry and convicted, realizing that I truly did not know the answer myself. Later that night, before falling asleep, I knelt down and earnestly pleaded with the Lord to transform my life. The very next day, something changed.

My girlfriend and I began attending my friend's grandmother's church. In that small congregation, I invited Christ into my life.

A Life-Changing Encounter with God

While singing in the choir before the pastor's sermon, I was suddenly overcome with a powerful spiritual sensation. Compelled by this overwhelming feeling, I stepped out from the choir, stood before the congregation, and declared sincerely, **"Today, I repent of my sins and**

receive Jesus Christ as my Lord and 'personal' Savior." The congregation erupted in applause, and then I felt the same spiritual power lift me. As someone who loved basketball, I began jumping high into the air and then gently landed on my back, where I started to shake. Instead of fear, I experienced a deep sense of peace and refreshment. When it was over, they told me I had been sanctified—cleansed and set apart. I cannot speak about anyone else's experience, but my life changed in an instant.

I immediately gave up smoking cigarettes, weed, drinking alcohol, cursing, hanging out, and womanizing—not as a requirement for becoming a Christian, but because I genuinely wanted my life to be different. The Lord transforms our lives according to our willingness and desire to change. This principle also applies to family relationships.

Personal Convictions and Christian Freedom

After seventeen years of striving to live a morally upright life, I eventually realized that the heart of my faith was the **Moral Law—the Ten Commandments**—fulfilled through love, as described in **Romans 13**. The main thing I needed to avoid was illicit sexual relationships.

Over time, I began to allow myself to drink casually to relax and to use mild cursing as a form of venting, never directed at anyone. Today, I continually pray for God to watch over my words so that I do not sin with my tongue, and I strive to live as the Lord convicts me, seeking a spiritually clean life. I am careful not to cause others to stumble because of my freedom.

In **I Corinthians 8**, the Apostle Paul addresses freedom in Christ, discussing issues like eating or abstaining from meat offered to idols. He teaches that such practices neither make us better nor worse before God, relegating them to personal conscience. Paul concludes in **verse 13**, *"Therefore, if [my eating a] food is a cause of my brother's falling or of hindering [his spiritual advancement], I will not eat [such] flesh forever, lest I cause my brother to be tripped up and fall and to be offended."* This means we must be sensitive to the spiritual maturity of others and avoid causing them to stumble.

The Importance of Not Judging Others

What Christians choose to do is a matter of personal conviction, varying from person to person based on spiritual growth. Our primary guide, prompted by the Spirit of God, is the **Moral Law** or the Ten Commandments that God's Spirit writes on the tablets of our hearts **(Jeremiah 31:31-34)**. We should not judge one another but rather admonish and encourage. **Romans 14:4** says, *"Who are you to pass judgment on and censure another's household servant? It is before his own master that he stands or falls. And he shall stand and be upheld, for the Master (the Lord) is mighty to support him and make him stand."*

Some people, due to past habits, cannot handle drinking without falling into drunkenness, while others can. The real issue is drunkenness and situations that lead to illicit relationships. **Romans 14:1-23** supports this perspective.

VI. New Beginnings and the Truth of Spiritual Gifts

The Reality of Divine Visions

As I moved forward in life, I experienced a significant transition. With financial support from my father to lodge for one week in a rooming house, I was able to leave my girlfriend's mother's house. From there, I enrolled in a community college with assistance from my employer and began sensing my call to ministry. This change marked a new chapter for me, both personally and spiritually.

My involvement with the Full Gospel Businessmen Fellowship International opened the door to deeper spiritual experiences. During a retreat in the Catskill Mountains, I encountered a profound outpouring of the Holy Spirit. In that moment, I spoke in tongues and received a vision of vast cotton fields. The scripture **Zechariah 4:6b** resonated strongly within me: *"...Not by might, nor by power, but by My Spirit [of Whom the oil is a symbol], says the Lord of hosts."* This spiritual revelation was later connected with "fields white unto harvest" in **John chapter four**, and I felt a distinct calling from God towards evangelism.

Visions from God are real for every generation until the coming of the Lord, then they will cease because we will see what we have been believing. In **Acts 2:17**, the Apostle Peter quotes the prophet Joel in **Joel 2:28**, *"And afterward I will pour out*

My Spirit upon all flesh; and your sons and your daughters shall prophesy, your old men shall dream dreams, your young men shall see visions." I've had visions throughout the span of my life, and this was the first.

—Why Some Don't Believe in Visions—

Cessationism is a traditional theological perspective rooted in translation hermeneutics and cultural interpretation. Originating from the teachings of John Calvin, this doctrine was adopted by Reformed Churches and some Baptist Churches. It holds that the **"miraculous"** spiritual gifts described in **I Corinthians 12:4-11**—such as speaking in tongues, prophecy, and healing—ceased in the Church after the canonization of Scripture.

According to cessationist theology, these spiritual gifts ended with the death of the last Apostle, most likely John. This conclusion is based on the belief that once the Early Church and the Apostles' mission were established, there was no longer a need for further revelation. The canonization and codification of Scripture, finalized as late as the 4th century and at the Council of Trent in 1546, are seen as the closing of God's revelatory work. Cessationists support their position using **Hebrews 1:1**, which states that what is recorded in Scripture is interpreted as God's final Word.

The Limitations of Translation and Interpretation

However, these conclusions are difficult to verify, as God's Word is both inspirational and revelatory, especially in how it reveals the meaning of the original languages.

Each translation of Scripture introduces subtle shifts in meaning, as words change from language to language. This linguistic truth underscores that spiritual gifts do not add to God's written Word. Instead, they disclose the depth and richness of the original languages, offering inspired guidance and direction to God's people.

The Continuation of Spiritual Gifts

In light of this, it can be concluded that spiritual gifts persist until the culmination of the ages. As stated in **I Corinthians 13:8-10**: *"Love never fails [never fades out or becomes obsolete or comes to an end]. As for prophecy (the gift of interpreting the divine will and purpose), it will be fulfilled and pass away; as for tongues, they will be destroyed and cease; as for knowledge, it will pass away [it will lose its value and be superseded by truth].*

For our knowledge is fragmentary (incomplete and imperfect), and our prophecy (our teaching) is fragmentary (incomplete and imperfect).

But when the complete and perfect (total) comes, the incomplete and imperfect will vanish away (become antiquated, void, and superseded).

This passage suggests that spiritual gifts remain necessary as long as humanity exists in a state of partial knowledge and incomplete revelation.

The Meaning of "Verity" in Scripture

The term **"Verity"** in this context is a biblical translation signifying something factual. In the Gospel of John, Jesus uses *"verily, verily"* to preface significant statements, emphasizing their truth. For example, in **John 14:12**, Jesus declares, *"I assure you, most solemnly I tell you, if anyone steadfastly believes in Me, he will himself be able to do the things that I do; and he will do even greater things than these, because I go to the Father."* This statement indicates that Jesus will send the Holy Spirit to empower believers for their mission, but not with messianic power. The adjective "Greater" modifies the "works" of Christ, regarding being in more places at once, not as more profound than the works of the Lord. But spiritual gifts will accompany them on their journey, as we see in **Mark 16:17-18,** which is ironically excluded in some translations. *"And these attesting signs will accompany those who believe: in My name they will drive out demons; they will speak in new languages; They will pick up serpents; and [even] if they drink anything deadly, it will not hurt them; they will lay their hands on the sick, and they will get well."*

The Importance of Spiritual Gifts for the Mission

God continues to send His Spirit to gift His people for the mission to which He has called them—The Great Commission **(Matthew 28:18-20)**. Without these spiritual gifts, the mission would lack direction and purpose. The enduring presence of spiritual gifts ensures that God's people are equipped for the work He intends them to do.

VII. Education, Opportunity, and Moving Forward

Through my changed life and relationships, I witnessed to my ex-girlfriend, my best friend girlfriend, a coworker, a classmate, a Jewish girl, and a young lady from my old neighborhood, all of whom came to Christ. I led my best friend to recommit to the Lord. My greatest joy was leading my wife to the Lord and seeing her filled with the Spirit.

After marriage, when we had our children, I led my daughters to the Lord at seven and eight, and my son when he was three years old. All of them requested it of their own volition. Since then, all my children have grown into morally and spiritually inclined adults, evading the stereotype of preachers' kids.

How it Started

When I was charged with assault during a pick-up basketball game in Central Park, Upstate, I was incarcerated in the County Jail for forty days. I was acquitted of the charges because I was innocent. My role in the altercation was a mere boxing match with a few light blows thrown. But the principal still expelled me before graduation.

Regardless of the circumstances that held me back, I believe that God used social programs such as **Affirmative Action** to open doors for me and others during a time of steep discrimination. It provided opportunities that would have otherwise been out of reach. This isn't an excuse to live a life without boundaries, but some young people living in scarce resources that create crime, violence, and immorality become products of their environment. While it helped many minorities, I believe today's generation must find new ways to rise without it, as it is sometimes viewed as reverse discrimination.

However, the difficulty within racial disparity—the state of being separate but equal—becomes a disparity within itself, based on quota filling. If the dominant culture sees the minority culture as being given benefits above them, they may perceive the minority as less qualified, and in their eyes, it becomes reverse discrimination. Consequently, the majority of qualified minorities may not get the jobs, positions, and education that they are qualified for. A viable solution that churches should take advantage of that I used throughout my pastorate was called Urban Community Development. It was an outreach to disadvantaged communities to empower people to create education opportunities, job placement, business start-ups, and home ownership opportunities. That's where many of my troubles in ministry began, because it was resisted as a whole, seen as a waste of resources to undeserving people.

But the Lord continued to guide my path. Although the principal expelled me in my senior year just before graduation due to an altercation during a basketball game, I completed the **CETA (Comprehensive Employment and Training Act)** program and earned my **GED**. Through the CETA program, I was trained in carpentry, electricity, and plumbing, and began working as a maintenance man at a children's shelter. The director noticed my rapport with the youth and encouraged me to enroll in Schenectady County Community College in Human Services, offering me a job working with the children.

During college, I asked my EOP counselor to arrange a summer co-op in Columbia, South Carolina, where I could also visit my mother. That summer, I met my wife, Doris, a nursing student at the University of South Carolina. We were married that summer in a courthouse, then married again in her family's church. We later returned to Schenectady, where we continued our education.

Just before my senior year at the College of Saint Rose, God led us back to South Carolina. There, I was licensed and ordained in an Afrocentric Methodist church, attended their Seminary, graduated in the Master of Divinity program, and began my pastoral ministry.

On Family, Forgiveness, and Letting Go of the Past

Before continuing, I want to acknowledge my parents. Although they were separated from me for much of my life, I never saw them with other partners, except my father in his later years, which I've mentioned. Outsiders may stand on the outside looking in and judge based on rumors and gossip, but only God truly knows each person's heart. Everyone has flaws, bad habits, and secrets. Only God can judge the secrets of the heart. If my parents had companionships during our separation, that is their private matter. The past cannot be changed, and any wrongs are **"water over the dam."** According to their faith and in God's book, as well as mine, they are forgiven. Any negative thoughts I had are now drowned in God's **"Sea of Forgetfulness,"** as described in **Micah 7:19**, **Psalm 103:12**, and **Hebrews 8:12**. I call this **"forever forgiveness."**

Memories, Hope, and a New Life in Christ

Our memories follow us, perhaps even into eternity. While tormented memories are a topic for another time, the good news is that in Christ and the coming glory on earth, only good memories will remain. **Revelation 21:14** promises that God will wipe away every tear and erase sorrow, crying, pain, and death. Since Scripture says we will know Abraham, Isaac, and Jacob in heaven, we will also know and remember one another with joy. It is important to remember that one negative can erase many positives, but one positive can also erase many negatives. There will be no negatives in glory.

Understanding the New Birth and Our Identity in Christ

After hearing the Gospel, when God's Spirit reveals Christ to our hearts and we invite Him in as our personal Savior, we experience the **"new birth"**—the indwelling of the Spirit and a new nature. From God's perspective, we are separated from our old life and begin a new life in Christ. God, who is too holy to look upon sin, sees us as He sees Christ: without sin. This does not mean believers cannot sin; rather, we are always forgiven through the atoning blood of Christ. God does not hold our sins against us, nor does He sever our relationship with Him. Sin may hinder our fellowship, but God never abandons us—He waits for us to repent and return.

New Life in Christ

It's important to remember that transformation in Christ is not about ignoring the past, which is denial, but about allowing God's grace to redefine our identity.

Sharing your testimony is a powerful witness of God's work, regardless of how others may respond. True change is evident not in what we leave behind, but in how we pursue what lies ahead.

II Corinthians 5:17, *"Therefore if any person is [ingrafted] in Christ (the Messiah) he is a new creation (a new creature altogether); the old [previous moral and spiritual condition] has passed away. Behold, the fresh and new has come!"*

A genuine believer cannot be judged based on their past life. However, that is the exact problem with testimonies among Pharisaic judgmental people. They take apart the person's testimony and use it against them, but don't let that stop you from sharing because we overcome by our testimonies **(Revelation 11:12)**. For example, take a look at the Apostle Paul. After his conversion on the Damascus Road, he was judged by Jews and Christians. Jews judged him as a Mosaic law nullifier and Christians judged him as their persecutor, but persecution was his past, and fulfilling the law was his present. He was a new man and had to prove himself. Proving ourselves is not about becoming "people pleasers." It is rather about maintaining our integrity before the Lord, and that truth will prevail over time. He writes about it in **Philippians 3:7-14**, but my concentration is on **verses 13-14.**

Paul isn't discrediting or denying his accomplishments in the passage. Rather, he is pointing out that his accomplishments from the past do not define him in the present. Whatever you were before Christ isn't who you are in Christ now. Pay close attention to **verses 13** and **14**: *"I do not consider, brethren, that I have captured and made it my own [yet]; but one thing I do [it is my one aspiration]: forgetting what lies behind and straining forward to what lies ahead, I press on toward the goal to win the [supreme and heavenly] prize to which God in Christ Jesus is calling us upward."*

VIII. Transformative Reflections

Early Life in Brooklyn and Schenectady

Growing up on the rough streets of Brooklyn and Schenectady, New York, during the 1950s, 60s, and 70s was like navigating a minefield. Each day presented challenges, and I strived to rise above the scarcity that surrounded my family and me. Despite my best intentions, trouble often seemed to find me, even though I never sought it out.

Influence of Family and Early Choices

I looked up to my brother Johnny as a mentor, but unfortunately, I learned many negative behaviors from him. At just eleven years old, I began spending time on the streets, drinking wine, and smoking cigarettes.

During my fifth-grade year, I was a straight-A student and a teacher's art pet. However, things changed when I turned twelve and transitioned to middle school. My brother's influence led me to become truant, causing me to miss a significant amount of school. As a result, I was held back a grade.

Moving to Schenectady and New Challenges

In 1964, my parents reconciled, and our family moved to Schenectady, New York, to be with my father. The environment there was more laid back and rural compared to Brooklyn. Because I was from Brooklyn, my new friends perceived me as a "bad guy," and I played into that image to gain their acceptance. Unfortunately, my pattern of truancy continued, and my friends and I often skipped school at my place while my father was at work. As a latchkey kid, I avoided truant officers by never letting them inside when they visited. Eventually, my truancy caught up with me, leading to my placement in juvenile detention through the courts.

Rehabilitation at Tryon School for Boys

I was sentenced to the Tryon School for Boys in Perth, New York. Today, Tryon is coed. It was located just outside the historic town of Johnstown in a rural community. Tryon was a pilot program launched by the state in 1966 to rehabilitate troubled juveniles without incarceration facilities that looked like prisons—there were no walls around us on the outside or bars inside, just cottages and open dorms.

I arrived that same year as the thirty-sixth boy admitted. Surprisingly, the program offered more freedom than I expected, and I quickly adapted to life there. I earned respect after a fight with our cottage bully. I won the fight, and we shook hands. I quickly made friends with the biggest guy in the place, a 6' 8" young man from the Bronx, and we played on the basketball team together. I worked in the dispensary and became an honors student. Years later, Mike Tyson would attend the same school, and his boxing coach had once been my basketball coach. He even wanted to become my legal guardian, hoping I would play high school basketball in Johnstown because of my athletic potential.

A Pivotal Summer and a Wake-Up Call

Tryon School for Boys was like a vacation away from home. We even held dances with the girls' school, and a priest would come once a month and serve us communion. We were all rehabilitating, but our behavior problems persisted. We would steal the wine from communion and laugh till we fell out on the floor.

Due to my good behavior and achievements, I earned the privilege to go home for two weeks that summer. My main motivation for returning was to see my girlfriend rather than my father.

After missing the bus back to Tryon, my father reluctantly paid for a cab to return me to school. On the way, the driver made inappropriate advances, placing his hand on my leg. As we were near Johnstown, I told him the school was waiting for me at the bus station, prompting him to remove his hand and drop me off. I don't know, but he could have been a molester or worse. What I do know is that God was with me. I safely contacted the school, and they picked me up. This unsettling incident made me reflect on my life choices and sparked thoughts about God. Not long after, I was granted early release and returned home to my father.

High School Years and a Life-Altering Incident

My basketball skills improved, and I joined my high school basketball team with hopes of attending college. However, during my senior year, an incident derailed those plans.

During a pickup game in Central Park in upstate New York, a fight broke out between my team and the opposing team. The altercation started with me and one of their players. We threw a few minor boxing blows. But his friends ran and left him. He then ran down a hill towards a pond. He was injured while running when one of my friends threw a stone that hit him in the head, then proceeded to beat him while he was down. Although my conscience prevented me from participating in the violence, we were all accessories to the crime and were arrested at school the following Monday. I was booked, jailed, and my father refused to bail me out. I spent forty days in county jail awaiting trial.

Turning Point after Incarceration

While incarcerated, my high school coach and a semi-pro basketball player—now a judge—helped secure my acquittal and release.

During my time in jail, I received a "Good News" Bible from a church's prison outreach and began to seriously consider embracing Christianity. Unfortunately, upon returning home, I was soon put out of the house by my father, without notice.

Carrying a garbage bag filled with my clothes, I braved a snowstorm to reach my girlfriend's house. **This marked the beginning of my spiritual journey and my path toward faith.**

Because of the incident, I was expelled from high school before graduation and lost my athletic scholarship to a Junior College downstate.

On the edge of homelessness and loneliness, I braved the path ahead of me, believing that God would rescue me.

IX. From Rock Bottom to Redemption

Question: *If I am what I have, what am I if it's lost?* Answer: Nothing, from the human perspective, but from the divine perspective, we remain significant in the sight of God, and God will provide and prosper those in Christ to rise. This is my story here.

The saying, **"When you are down, the only way is up**," holds a profound truth: reaching the lowest point in life actually leaves us with two choices—to rise above our circumstances or perish and drift away. With God's help, it is possible to overcome even the darkest moments.

In 1973, after enduring three years of debilitating and spiraling existence, I experienced my second vision, which marked a turning point.

Following a late-night encounter with a notorious drug dealer at a local nightclub and bar alongside my girlfriend, I was offered the chance to sell drugs. After the meeting, we spent the night at a Holiday Inn. While "shacked up" there, I fell into a deep sleep and had a vivid dream. In the dream, I found myself outside in a storm, trying to reach a white house. As I approached the house, an audible voice called my name three times, "Jarvis, Jarvis, Jarvis." Startled, I woke up and looked for my girlfriend, but she was fast asleep. Overwhelmed by a presence, I returned to sleep. From that moment, for the next year, I began reading the Bible from Genesis, using the copy I had received while in jail. Through this journey, I learned what it meant to become a Christian. My primary concern became transforming my life through Christ, with heaven being a given.

During that time, it felt like the answer to my dilemma was behind the four walls of some church. But my natural senses registered "unwelcome" in my conscience, because I didn't feel like I was good enough. Besides, I saw churches like relics of a museum. Yet, I still sensed that God's hand was guiding me, and I felt like a soldier on a mission. I even found myself preaching about the Lord in bars after becoming intoxicated, and would read the Bible at home until I sobered up. Some people thought I was losing my mind.

Eventually, my girlfriend and I secured good jobs and moved into a very nice apartment. We held a gathering there and engaged in a conversation about being "saved." At the time, none of us were Christians. Years later, I looked back and remembered a peaceful presence at the gathering, reflecting on Christ's words in **Luke 19:10**: ***"For the Son of Man came to seek and to save that which was lost."*** I also recalled **John 6:44a**: ***"No one is able to come to me unless the Father Who sent Me attracts and draws him and gives him the desire to come to Me..."*** In that moment, I realized it was the Lord at our gathering.

I accepted the Lord as my personal Savior at a small Pentecostal church. I told my girlfriend that we could no longer live together, choosing to abstain from sex. I left and moved into a rooming house. From there, I enrolled in college, balanced coursework, played on the basketball team, cleaned offices in the evenings, and even drove a cab for a short period.

The Lord Raised Me

Looking back, I often wonder how my life might have turned out differently if I had received parental guidance. In many ways, it felt as if the Lord was literally raising me again, a process I think of as discipleship.

During this time, I helped my best friend recommit his life to the Lord. He had accepted Christ at age twelve. His grandmother, an elderly woman who mentored me, invited me to live with them. She recognized genuine transformation in me, and her intention was for me to help her grandson stay on the "straight and narrow." However, the lifestyle I observed in her church—a small Pentecostal congregation—did not align with the Christian life described in the Bible. Since I was not raised in the church and wasn't indoctrinated with traditional doctrine, I witnessed God's grace in salvation and a normal lifestyle, avoiding violations of the moral law written on our hearts by the Spirit of God. Eventually, I left during my co-op internship for South Carolina.

During that summer stay with my mother in South Carolina, while working at a camp near Columbia, I met my wife.

I was one of two camp directors, and she was a counselor on her co-op from the University of South Carolina Nursing School. We connected and began dating.

One night, after a bowling date, we stood in her yard and kissed before she went inside. In that moment, I felt the presence of the Lord come upon us, and I knew she was a gift from God. After getting to know each other for only three months, I asked her to marry me, and she said yes. Despite our apprehension about our parents' consent due to the short period we had known each other; we decided to elope. Later, we were married again at her church and returned to Schenectady, NY, to continue our education.

I was an up-and-coming star athlete on the team at the College of Saint Rose in Albany, NY, but sacrificed the possibilities of my future as a basketball player for my call to ministry. We stayed there for one year before feeling God's call to return to South Carolina to raise our family and begin ministry.

A Third Vision: Turning Point

Just before I returned to Schenectady, NY, after my summer co-op, I experienced my third vision. It happened one Saturday morning as I lay half asleep in my nephew's bed, which was situated across from the kitchen. In that moment, I slipped into what felt like sleep paralysis. It was marked by a sense of peace and calm. I could actually see my mother in the kitchen, but then her image slowly faded away. Suddenly, I was presented with a fourfold panoramic vision, unfolding like a slideshow before my eyes.

The Fourfold Vision

The first scene revealed me inside a box-like structure, with a huge angel leaning over the box. The angel was looking down at me, speaking in what I sensed was the Hebrew language. In the second scene, a scroll levitated in the air, also written in Hebrew. The third scene showed numerous people, all dressed in multicolored T-shirts. The fourth and final scene depicted me kneeling beside a stool next to a grand piano in a mansion-like room. Above my head, I could hear what I believed were angels singing in perfect harmony: "Give the Lord a day, give the Lord a day, give the Lord a day."

After emerging from the vision, I spent time prayerfully reflecting on its meaning. My conclusion was that the Lord was calling me toward a multiethnic, cross-cultural ministry. This calling would require me to study the original Hebrew language and to dedicate myself fully to the task.

Looking back, I recognize that this vision was partially fulfilled in 2004, when I began working in racial reconciliation ministry across cultures. I will share more about that experience in the upcoming sections. However, I believe the vision has not yet been completely fulfilled. I remain confident that it will be, because God's Will always prevails.

Stage II: Confronting & Growing through Church Conflicts

X. Trials of Testimony—Spiritual Growth Through Adversity

Here, we explore and navigate the second stage to wholeness through the purpose of trouble, spiritual resistance, and the value of testimonies.

The Purpose of Trouble

The Apostle Paul's reflection on his **"thorn in the flesh"** in **II Corinthians 12:7-10** provides a foundational understanding of how trouble and adversity can shape the life of a disciple. Paul describes his affliction—believed to be a debilitating eye condition as a result of severe persecution that required him to be guided by others—as a **"messenger of Satan to buffet him,"** implying physical pain. This persistent trouble, according to Paul, served a divine purpose: it kept him humble in light of the numerous revelations he received from God. This principle forms the core of my perspective: **Trouble acts as an agent that refines and strengthens the character of those who follow the Lord**.

Risky Testimonies

Openly sharing our testimonies is an act of vulnerability. When we choose to reveal our personal experiences, we also risk exposing ourselves to the judgments and opinions of others. This openness can sometimes invite criticism, even from those closest to us, such as family members.

Jesus Warns Against Judgmental Attitudes

In **Matthew 7:1-5**, Jesus cautions against adopting a judgmental attitude toward others. He uses the analogy of a "lent"—a small fault—found in another's eye, which is judged by someone who actually has a "splinter"—a much greater flaw—in their own eye. The comparison highlights that the person passing judgment is often overlooking their own larger issues while focusing on minor faults in others to distract attention away from their own bigger fault. It's called **reverse psychology,** and in modern terms, it's called **gaslighting**. Families must cease gaslighting, especially when they have similar problems. Instead, they should become more empathetic because they share a common problem.

Jesus' teaching serves as a reminder that judgmental people, especially in religious contexts, often become faultfinders. They intentionally seek faults in others to distract others from their own, often more significant problems. This act of judgment is a way for them to feel better about themselves, shifting attention away from their personal struggles. He refers to them as a fault-finding generation **(Matthew 16:4)**.

—The Challenge of Testimonies—

Challenges in a New Pastorate

When I transitioned to my third pastorate, I encountered further trials. During a heated leaders' meeting about outreach to the community, one leader publicly attributed my success to my background, labeling me as a Brooklyn "N" word due to testimonies I shared. This comment not only reflected prejudice but also altered how others viewed my efforts and character. It touched a sensitive button in me, because of where I came from, that almost moved me to an altercation, immediately intervened in by the other leaders. But I know my limits. I would never have gotten into a fight with him, but I would have defended myself.

Challenges at a Eurocentric Church

During my time serving in an affluent Eurocentric church, I noticed that some members believed the sermon was focused on my personal experiences. In reality, my testimony was only a small part of the message. Despite this, it became a point of reference for some, shaping their perceptions of me and the sermon itself.

Recapping the Journey—Early Ministry Experiences

After moving back to South Carolina, my family and I lived with my mother-in-law for six months while I worked at an adult disability center. Our first child, Jeremy, was born during this time. I was ordained and began pastoring a small country church characterized by a white plank building, heated by kerosene during the winter months.

The environment was not welcoming, and from my very first sermon to the abrupt cancellation of my first members meeting (due to arguments about the previous pastor), I sensed a deep tension within the congregation. The former pastor's continued presence only intensified the unease.

My wife and I returned home after that first day, both surprised and unprepared for the reality of church life. I didn't grow up in the church, so I had entered ministry with ideals shaped by Scripture, only to realize that churches often develop from the traditions and concepts of their founders rather than directly from the biblical model. Despite our reservations, we stayed for a year and a half. During that time, I enrolled in the church's seminary to further my education while continuing to serve as pastor.

The church grew, particularly among youth, yet I faced resistance when advocating for financial accountability, such as keeping church funds in a bank instead of at the treasurer's house. My compensation was a mere $75 every two weeks in cash, and I commuted long distances between home, church, and seminary until I was reassigned to another congregation and entered seminary full-time.

Seminary and New Opportunities

In 1979-80, my wife, our young son, and I moved into the seminary while I continued pastoring. As an assistant dorm director at the seminary, I witnessed behaviors inconsistent with Christian values, yet my faith remained steady even as some students left due to their experiences. I developed a close friendship with another preacher and his wife, and our conversations about evangelism proved uplifting and productive. Simultaneously, I was offered the opportunity to pastor another church near the seminary—a congregation of about 90 that grew nearly to capacity under my leadership. However, challenges remained.

Much of the leadership was involved in the Masons, which made me uneasy because I saw them as a secret society, and there is no secret in God. After life mysteries, yes, but church reality, no. From my studies of God's Word, the secrets of the Kingdom of God and the Church are not withheld from the people. The Book of Ephesians reveals those mysteries.

Despite the church's growth, I had to supplement our income by working at a local Knitting Mill and selling vacuum cleaners, as my wife was unable to work due to two miscarriages. I also moonlighted by doing minor house upgrades, from painting and roofing.

During this period, rumors about my past began to circulate among the congregation due to my testimonies. Nevertheless, I remained committed to both preaching and shepherding the flock.

Trials of Integrity—Character Development

One evening, after returning from my job at the Knitting Mill, my wife informed me that a parishioner—an emotional female member—wanted to see me. Because of the trust and closeness in my marriage, I asked my wife if she wanted to accompany me, but she declined, believing the woman might not open up with her present. Upon arriving, I found myself in a potentially compromising situation: the woman wore a sheer blouse, served dinner, and had the Playboy channel on TV. After dinner, she served me tea in a manner that revealed her intent. Rather than act on the situation, I prayed with her, demonstrating respect and integrity. She later expressed gratitude, telling me I was the first pastor to treat her with such dignity. She became a steady member and friend to both my wife and me, and I continued to minister to her family, including her brother in prison. There were other incidents with women in the church that I don't have time to share here, but like Joseph, I departed from the temptation.

Facing Tradition and Pursuing Reform

During my tenure at the new church, we demolished an old building next to the new facility to create additional parking space. To my surprise, many members wept and collected bricks, believing the Holy Spirit resided in that old structure. This experience underscored the deep attachment many have to tradition and physical spaces, rather than seeing the church as the Body of Christ. I realized that meaningful reform in a traditional church would require significant changes in leadership and membership, a challenge I was not yet ready to meet. I remained until I graduated from seminary in 1984 and then accepted a new pastoral charge at the request of my friend across from me at the seminary.

XI. A New City & Pentecostal Explosion

After graduating from seminary in 1984, my wife, son, and daughter relocated with me to a new city in Tennessee. We settled into the parsonage that sat next door to the church, a location that naturally led to frequent visitors and regular activity around our home.

As I entered my third pastorate, I had matured both emotionally and spiritually, developing a deeper understanding of church life and its complexities. Despite this personal growth, I found that stories from my past continued to shape how others perceived me. Persistent stereotypes and misunderstandings about my character followed me, causing moments of humiliation and discouragement. This was particularly difficult since I had not grown up in the church and had approached ministry with strong scriptural ideals.

Welcome to the New Pastorate

Our journey to the new pastorate began on a Saturday evening in the warmth of fall. We arrived in our car, accompanied by a moving truck. The church members gathered to greet us, offering both their hands and their hearts as they helped unload our belongings. Their generosity extended beyond physical assistance; they warmly invited us to a welcome dinner held at the church next door, allowing us to feel instantly at home within the community.

First Sermons and Vision

On our first Sunday, I delivered a sermon titled **"Where Do We Go from Here**." The congregation responded thoughtfully, and their smiles reassured me of their support. I typically preach in series to provide the depth and detail needed for listeners to understand God's direction for their lives, so I continued with part two the following Sunday.

The Saturday before the third Sunday brought a profound spiritual experience. I had a vivid vision of an angel standing at the foot of my bed. The angel appeared androgynous, with a light complexion, long curly black hair, and dressed in a robe radiating a white-like glow. The angel extended its hand toward me, filling the room with a peaceful presence. As I reached to touch the angel's hand in my spirit, I felt a surge of energy, like electricity, flowing up my arm into my chest. The vision concluded, and I prepared for church, carrying its impact with me.

That Sunday, I preached a sermon entitled **"Endless Love**," drawing from **Hosea 1:2-3**, where God commands Hosea to take a wife of unfaithfulness as a symbol of Israel's relationship with the Lord. I also incorporated an analogy from the movie of the same name to further illustrate the message. The Spirit of God moved powerfully during the service, prompting spontaneous praise throughout the congregation. The previous pastor's radio broadcast, which I had inherited, extended the reach of the sermon across the city. Another pastor heard the message and promoted it, which sparked significant growth in our church community.

Rapid Growth and Expansion

Between 1984 and 1987, our worship attendance surged from roughly 90 to 250 and then to about 400. As crowds grew, we added chairs down the aisles and set up a closed-circuit system downstairs to accommodate the overflow. The enthusiasm was so great that people from the neighborhood would run to church to secure a seat. In response, we opened the church doors to those unable to find a seat, allowing them to listen to the service from their cars or on the lawn. This overwhelming response made it clear that a larger facility was urgently needed.

At the close of these three years, we learned that a nearby Southern Baptist Church, less than a quarter mile away, planned to relocate and was preparing to sell its property. The facility included a sanctuary with seating for a thousand, a chapel, around fifty rooms, an industrial kitchen, a fellowship hall, a children's wing, and spacious offices. We entered into negotiations, secured the property, and moved into the new church in 1988.

Continued Growth and Ministry Initiatives

Within a year of moving, our congregation expanded to approximately 700 members, with about 400 participating in Sunday School. I began leading weekly marriage and family seminars in the chapel and organized men's prayer meetings that grew so large they spilled out into the hall. The Married Couples' Ministry and Singles Ministry became central to our growth strategy. We also formed interpretive dance teams—well before such ministries gained wider popularity.

Our outreach evangelism efforts played a crucial role in accelerating our growth. We focused on serving the poor and those living in disadvantaged communities, often referred to as "the hood" and project communities, organizing "back to school" block parties, equipping and preparing them for school. While this approach was a driving force behind our rapid expansion, it also generated some conflict with certain leaders and affluent members due to the focus on marginalized groups.

—*Is Reaching the Poor a Problem*—

We grew up poor during our formative years, but I never saw myself as poor, needy, yes, but not poor. For me, it was not a denial of my circumstances. Instead, it was a mindset to motivate me to meet my needs. Minus the crime element, I believe the majority of poor people desire to change their circumstances by striving to do better. But they become stereotyped through monolithic language and are all seen as bad people because of the behavior of a few.

The ministry of Christ was foretold in prophetic Scripture as being directed toward the poor, oppressed, and disenfranchised. In **Luke 4:18**, it is declared, ***"The Spirit of the Lord [is] upon Me, because He has anointed Me [the Anointed One, the Messiah] to preach the good news (the Gospel) to the poor; He has sent Me to announce release to the captives and recovery of sight to the blind, to send forth as delivered those who are oppressed*** *[who are downtrodden, bruised, crushed, and broken down by calamity]."* This emphasis on the poor is evident throughout both the Old and New Testaments, indicating that they are a vital part of God's plan for redemption and restoration.

The restoration of the ten lost tribes of Israel and the eventual Second Coming of Christ are closely intertwined with God's outreach to the poor. **Romans 11** would need in-depth analysis to fully understand this connection. If reaching the poor is central to God's plan, then spiritual resistance would naturally arise to hinder these efforts. In society, this resistance is often reflected as skepticism or apathy toward helping the poor, who are frequently stereotyped as undeserving or as a drain on public resources.

A troubling question arises: Why do some Christians, who are called to love, share this dismissive attitude? The answer may lie in the historical influence of the Puritan Ethic, which has shaped broad church culture and broader Christendom. This ethic teaches that poverty is a curse and wealth is a blessing, making outreach to the poor challenging both religiously and politically, especially when it involves incorporating poor individuals into church membership. Ultimately, this reveals a conflict between the haves and the have-nots.

The Puritan Ethic

The roots of the Puritan Ethic trace back to the early colonial Puritans. Their journey from feudal societies—where the majority were poor serfs under the authority of the crown and the pope—influenced their beliefs about wealth and poverty.

Poverty was seen not just as a curse, but as a possible sign of moral failure and divine displeasure. In contrast, the wealthy were considered morally upright and favored by God.

The Puritans believed that wealth was a reward for those who lived righteously, and that poverty resulted from a lack of divine favor and poor personal conduct, and the lack of a work ethic. Social problems such as crime and violence were attributed to poverty, which was viewed as a blight to be eradicated from both society and religion. This way of thinking persists today in church circles and American culture through Judeo/Christian doctrine, contributing to the perception that funding programs for the poor is a misuse of public money.

Conversely, the Prosperity Gospel movement teaches that wealth is the direct result of faith and giving. However, the poor rarely attend these churches due to their financial struggles, which are seen as consequences of poor stewardship and lack of personal responsibility. Prosperity is considered a sign of God's favor, yet true outreach to the poor requires unconditional grace—favor that is unmerited and sacrificial.

Personal Experience: Reaching the Poor

When I began evangelizing among the poor, my motivation did not stem from either the Puritan Ethic or the Prosperity Gospel. Instead, I was moved by God's love for His harvest. This approach, however, led to rumors and gossip within the church and ultimately resulted in some long-term members seeking my removal. The blame for this situation was rooted in the stories of my own upbringing in poverty. I compare it to the life of Christ as He ministered to common people, referred to as sinners. He was labeled a friend of sinners by the religious community and worse, as the prince of the devils **(Matthew 9:34)**.

XII. Spiritual Warfare: A Personal Reflection

Welcome to Spiritual Warfare. This section shares my personal journey and observations regarding spiritual battles experienced both in relationships and within a community context as a result of my testimonies.

I was not truly aware of the concept of spiritual warfare until I moved to a new city and took on new responsibilities as a pastor. The experiences I encountered in this environment have triggered memories of earlier events in my life that, in retrospect, were also manifestations of spiritual warfare.

In 1978, while in the Catskill Mountains, I received my call to the Ministry of Evangelism. Upon returning, I shared this revelation with my pastor, who affirmed my calling and officially licensed both me and my best friend as preachers.

One Sunday afternoon, as I sat in the pulpit listening to a visiting evangelist, I felt a deep sense of unease about his message. He was delivering a dogmatic sermon that condemned women, yet he presented himself as an attractive man who exuded sexuality. At the end of his sermon, he made an altar call, and four women responded, taking seats at the front. As the evangelist descended from the pulpit, I saw a dark, shadowy figure emerge from him and move toward the women. When it reached one woman, she slid from her chair to the floor, shaking. The congregation interpreted this as the Holy Spirit at work, but internally, I sensed it was an "unclean spirit of lust." I concluded privately that this incident could potentially lead to inappropriate interactions between the evangelist and the woman.

Personal Spiritual Battles

I also witnessed spiritual conflict in the lives of those close to me—my best friend and my girlfriend. My best friend, who had professed faith as a child and later reaffirmed his commitment, experienced a sudden seizure-like episode in our home. While others hesitated, I laid hands on him and rebuked the devil. Each time I touched him, I felt a lump move in his body, which I interpreted as a sign of spiritual oppression rather than possession, since I do not believe the Holy Spirit and a demon can coexist within a believer. When he recovered, he described a vision of hell. Tragically, years later, he passed away in his forties due to asphyxiation from a drug-induced high.

Deliverance from a Harmful Relationship

During a significant chapter of my life, I led my girlfriend to Christ. Following her conversion, she seemed to undergo a miraculous transformation, turning entirely away from her previous lifestyle. Formerly, she was deeply involved in sexual immorality, excessive drinking, and unruly behavior. At one stage, I considered marrying her, but after praying earnestly the night before our courthouse wedding, I felt the Lord speak to my spirit, making it clear that she was not meant to be my wife. Heeding this divine direction, I called off the wedding the next day, and we did not see each other for quite some time.

Our paths crossed again when she came to our house seeking help, having returned to her old ways with even greater intensity. My friend and I prayed for her and laid hands on her, but she responded with animalistic behavior, sliding to the floor and growling. After our prayers yielded no visible change, I took her back to her home. Upon arrival, her behavior persisted—she slid to the floor of the passenger seat like a snake. Unable to help further, I let her out and never saw her again, except for reading about her involvement in a domestically abusive relationship in the newspaper. Unfortunately, she died in her mid-forties from sclerosis of the liver from excessive alcohol consumption.

But when the unclean spirit has gone out of a man, it roams through dry [arid] places in search of rest, but it does not find any.

Then it says, I will go back to my house from which I came out. And when it arrives, it finds the place unoccupied, swept, put in order, and decorated.

Then it goes and brings with it seven other spirits more wicked than itself, and they go in and make their home there. And the last condition of that man becomes worse than the first. So also shall it be with this wicked generation **(Matthew 12:43-45)**.

Reflecting on these events, I believe God rescued and delivered me from what could have been a disastrous relationship. My only conclusion is that some individuals may pretend to accept the Lord or remain under spiritual oppression as believers, continuing unchanged in their old lifestyles and the Lord will take them home prematurely.

Spiritual Oppression and Domination in the Community

My experiences in this city extended well beyond personal relationships. I came to discern that negative spiritual influences had lingered over a section of the city and the community I served. I attributed this oppression to historical, unrepentant, unconfessed indiscretions, especially among local pastors, which built up, over time, like sweeping trash under the rug. Scripture says, *"A little leaven (a slight inclination to error, or a few false teachers) leavens the whole lump [it perverts the whole conception of faith or misleads the whole church]"* **(Galatians 5:9)**. I've learned that over time, past sins can become a stronghold, influencing individuals and communities when they are not dealt with.

In my view, experience and studies, these influences became a stronghold of sexual immorality that's difficult to break due to spreading patterns. Eventually, I identified this oppressive spirit as Dagon—the spirit of time past—keeping churches and communities focused on former days rather than the present, fostering pessimism. When sinful activity is concealed and justified, and rationalized as normal, it becomes a generational stronghold within families. The enemy uses these strongholds to attack relationships within both the church and families, ultimately stifling the church's mission in the community.

These insights are challenging to accept, as they require spiritual discernment beyond natural senses.

Understanding and Dismantling Strongholds

I identified the stronghold with what Christ described as the **"Strongman"** in **Matthew 12:29**: *"Or how can a person go into a strong man's house and carry off his goods (the entire equipment of his house) without first binding the strong man? Then indeed he may plunder his house."*

The strongman signifies a geographical principality, as referenced in **Ephesians 6:10-12** and **Daniel 10**, and overcoming it requires leaders in that area to unite in spiritual warfare **(Matthew 18:18-20)**. Together, they must dismantle the stronghold and drive out the strongman. However, if local leaders themselves are held as spiritual hostages by unconfessed and unrepentant sin, their efforts are rendered ineffective like the Seven sons of Sceva in **Acts 19:11-20**.

I have used a visual illustration of what it looks like for those harboring a sinful life from **II Timothy 2:25-26**: *"He must correct his opponents with courtesy and gentleness, in the hope that God may grant that they will repent and come to know the Truth [that they will perceive and recognize and become accurately acquainted with and acknowledge it], And that they may come to their senses [and] escape out of the snare of the devil, having been held captive by him, [henceforth] to do His [God's] will."*

The person held in bondage is ineffective in the work of Christ because they are paralyzed with fear that they will be exposed, so they compromise their faith and integrity and do not address sinful issues in others. To picture what is happening spiritually, it's like the spirit of condemnation holds a sign of condemnation over their head, impacting their conscience with guilt. To get free from the bondage, the passage above says they must acknowledge the error of their ways, repent, and embrace the truth through admonition from a leader with integrity **(James 5:16)** who will keep their situation confidential. When that happens, the blood of Christ's atonement judicially covers the person, and the spirit of condemnation departs, and the person is released and renewed.

XIII. Phenomenal Church Growth & Spiritual Opposition

At the outset of my ministry, my understanding of spiritual warfare was limited. I believed that churches and Christian communities were largely insulated from the influence of evil spirits. Yet, contrary to my initial perceptions, there was a distinct sense of spiritual opposition. Despite these challenges, God's anointing and the power of His Word were instrumental in driving remarkable church growth in the area.

With the growth of the church came unexpected difficulties. Several incidents sparked rumors that accused me of moral indiscretions, including allegations related to finances and inappropriate relationships. These rumors circulated rapidly, reaching the highest levels of church leadership. The resulting suspicion affected not only my personal reputation but also cast a shadow over the entire congregation. This atmosphere of distrust began to alter the tone of worship services and the spiritual climate within the church.

As gossip and judgment spread, the effects became increasingly evident. Church attendance declined significantly, and the once vibrant community that had been built on unity and spiritual growth found itself struggling under the weight of doubt and rumor. This experience underscored how destructive gossip and judgment can be within a faith community, as the decline in attendance became a tangible sign of these negative forces at work.

Escalation of Conflict and Personal Struggle

The lies and rumors continued to escalate, reaching the church hierarchy and resulting in my leadership being questioned. Allegations of sexual indiscretion and misappropriation of church funds were raised, despite being completely unfounded and unsupported by evidence. These challenges proved to be even more harrowing than those I had faced before my conversion.

In the midst of these trials, I resolved not to abandon my calling. However, the situation deteriorated into lawsuits, name-calling, threatening phone calls, and even acts of vandalism such as egg-throwing at the parsonage. The emotional toll was compounded by concerns for my three children. Faced with these pressures, I confided in my wife that if, by God's grace, I could not change the church, the church would inevitably change me. After much prayer, we decided to plan our departure.

Decision to Go Independent

Upon learning of a forthcoming lawsuit and the intention to remove me from the church and replace me with another pastor, I prayerfully chose not to abandon the vision for which God had called me to serve in that community. I convened a meeting with the church members to discuss the possibility of becoming independent. Just before concluding the vote to go independent, a primary leader in the denomination and other pastors sought to stop the vote, accompanied by the local police. Nonetheless, we succeeded.

The majority were in favor, but a group opposed the move, viewing the church building as my personal triumph. The matter went to court, where the judge ruled in favor of the former church members. As a result, my wife and children were required to leave the parsonage immediately.

A Nomadic Church Finds Its Way

Despite these setbacks, a substantial portion of the congregation remained with us. We became a nomadic church, worshipping in various locations, including two gymnasiums and a high school auditorium. Our numbers continued to grow, reaching 300 strong—an echo of Gideon's 300, who achieved victory against overwhelming odds. The final chapter of our journey unfolded unexpectedly.

One day, while driving near my home, I felt a strong inner prompting to stop at a nearby plant nursery. I parked, stepped out, and raised my hands in prayer, simply asking, "Lord, give us this land." Two weeks later, my cross-cultural partner and I met with the owners and, without a bank loan, secured 22.7 acres of prime land close to our outreach community.

—New Beginnings and Continued Growth—

With the support of the church membership, we dedicated the land, erected a tent, and worshipped there for six weeks despite challenging weather conditions. Attendance was so high that there was only standing room available, and many people came to Christ and joined the church, marking a new era of growth and outreach for our community. I declared that those who stayed with the church through the ordeals were desert babies, meaning their faith, like the Joshua generation, was strong, born out of adversity.

Flourishing Ministry

From 1989 to 1993, the new church continued to grow exponentially as a community church. We purchased a ranch-style house that sat on the land we bought and converted it into an office and fellowship space. My office and small staff were located along an adjacent boulevard. There was an immediate need to replace worship in a tent, so we constructed a modular building that accommodated 400 in worship and a larger fellowship space that we also used for other events.

As we grew as a congregation, so did our outreach to disadvantaged communities. We changed the name of Prayer Meeting and Bible Study on Wednesday nights to Discipleship Service to shift thinking to focus on our adjacent community. So once a month, we took the service to a gymnasium in a project community. Our dance team and gospel rap group performed, and someone would share a brief testimony. Afterward, we would dine together and canvass the crowd for our small discipleship teams, going into their homes once a week for Bible study and assessing their financial needs. Through our affluent suburban partner church, we established what we referred to as spiritual adoption, which would help them with financial discipline and budgeting, and contribute to their needs.

Through collaboration with the leaders, I started a nonprofit outreach ministry called Christian Cultural Ministries. The purpose was to supplement projects and programs that churches weren't accustomed to. One example was my "Bonded Father & Son Work Enrichment Program" designed to take teenagers through five steps toward academic achievement and community involvement. The difference was it would provide financial incentives for them. We added a teenage girl to the program who was failing in school, and her grades went from "D's" and "F's" to "A's" and "B's."

These efforts not only deepened relationships within the congregation but also strengthened the church's ties with the broader community, fostering a spirit of unity and service that became a defining feature of the ministry.

Church and Community Events Kick Off

Our racial reconciliation ministry expanded rapidly across the city and into different states. We organized play productions and special holiday events that drew the community into the church. Unchurched people started attending our worship services and accepted Christ.

Through racial reconciliation, we partnered with an affluent suburban church that joined us in our plans to construct what we called our Family Life Center, where we would worship and conduct a variety of events for the church and community.

It was a 1.2-million-dollar facility where we could worship and convert it to a basketball court, where we held weekly basketball leagues with the community. One event focused on local police and troubled men from the community playing against each other and reconciling. The building would house computer labs, recreational rooms for workouts, a large kitchen, and rooms for specialized music ministry. Our play productions expanded, even to a performance theater, and we held networking business expos with the community and large holiday events.

We then turned another corner. Throughout this period of flourishing, the church also faced intense spiritual opposition from disgruntled members of the community who saw our progress as bringing in unwanted people into the community. Some called them Riffraff. One example is our partnership with my cross-cultural partner's leadership foundation. Eventually, after convincing the community, we built 12 mixed-income houses on seven acres of our land, Fellowship Place. People who had not previously qualified for home ownership were able to purchase their first home.

XIV. Spiritual Attack: A Testimony and Call to Spiritual Readiness

Through my journey in ministry, I have witnessed how spiritual strongholds can hinder the work of the Church and oppose the spread of the Gospel. This battle is not new—it began in the earliest days of God's people and continues today. To advance God's Kingdom, we must recognize and confront these spiritual obstacles.

The ministry's efforts in racial reconciliation and outreach to disadvantaged communities drew attention and created opportunities for sharing the Gospel. However, they were also accompanied by personal spiritual challenges.

I experienced a season of personal struggle, reflecting my identity before accepting Christ. Looking back over my past, I asked myself, "Was I a good man?" When I didn't see the changes in leadership lifestyles, I began to think to myself, my ministry is useless. A midlife crisis and feelings of failure accompanied it. After seventeen years of faithfulness, I fell into a trap of infidelity. This statement does not excuse my failure. It points out that those who are engaged in spiritual battle against the enemy become targets of Satan, using his arsenal to disable them, which is launched by a "seducing spirit" that deceives.

In a spirit of transparency, despite those who knew and wanted to keep it secret, I took full responsibility for my role. I confessed my infidelity to my wife, church leaders, and congregation, choosing honesty over secrecy despite concerns that it might disrupt the church's work. While forgiveness was found, the consequences of these actions continued to be felt, and I saw the affair as a spiritual setup and trap that I fell into.

The experience of unfaithfulness was likened to disturbing a hornet's nest—provoking spiritual attacks that targeted my core convictions and faithfulness to the Lord, my wife and family, and ministry. Let me put it in perspective:

Through my mother's biblical encouragement, I've never been a man driven by sex. Women who encountered me seductively before and after Christ can attest to that, but people don't excuse mistakes; fortunately, God forgives. The truth is, 80-90 percent of the women that I've been with before Christ, I refused to have sex with. When I met my wife, we abstained from sex before marriage. When I was stung, it awakened an adolescent desire that I felt I had missed. After the incident, I struggled with the desire until 2009. In 2009, I was delivered from the sting of the devil, a story that I will share coming up.

The adversary, described as the "accuser of the brethren" (Revelation 12:10), sought to undermine my confidence and dedication and ruin my reputation, and slandered me before God as no better than the failures of pastors before me.

Becoming Authentic and Vulnerable

This period, in 1994, recapped, brought to light personal struggles with depression, loneliness, and generational patterns from my male heritage. I felt unloved, both at home and in ministry. These feelings culminated in the affair during a time of heavy church involvement. Seeking affirmation and love, my vulnerability led to a relationship with a young woman in the church who told me everything I wanted to hear and expressed her love for me. Following this event, I made profound changes, stepping down from an idealized image, shedding pretense, and embracing authenticity—shaved my head, got a tattoo, and an earring in my ear. The tattoo was of our outreach cross logo, and the earring was a small cross. The symbolism for me represented "passion and pain." Later, that proved to be a phase, and I shed the earring.

Together with the congregation, I began studying "This Present Darkness" by Frank Peretti, which deepened the church's understanding of spiritual warfare. This process encouraged greater honesty and openness within the church community and intercessory prayer ministry, even amid ongoing criticism. The congregation became more authentically engaged with the surrounding community, shedding religious pretenses and fostering genuine relationships.

Lessons Learned

This journey underscored the reality of spiritual warfare, which has become a primary focus of my ministry, alongside my current study of predictive prophecy. The narrative of Job is a reminder that life's trials and temptations serve a greater purpose. When confronted with temptation, failure requires one to repeat the test; however, perseverance and success lead to higher levels of accountability and blessings from the Lord.

Today, I encourage individuals and churches to equip themselves with the full armor of God, practice spiritual discipline, and cultivate the fruit of the Spirit. Foundational scriptural passages—Ephesians 6:10-18, 2 Corinthians 10:3-5, and Galatians 5:22-23—serve as guiding principles, urging all to stand firm, take every thought captive, and embody the fruit of the Spirit in daily life.

XV. 2004—A Defining Visionary Year

Ministry Growth and Racial Reconciliation (1994–2002)

After my confession in 1994, our church faced challenges as some leaders and members chose to leave. However, the majority stayed, and some found the courage to confess their own indiscretions through our newly launched ministry, "Breaking the Yoke."

Over the next eight years, our ministry experienced steady growth. We established a reconciled relationship with a Eurocentric suburban church, which played a vital role in fundraising for our Family Life Center. This partnership was built upon a series of successful racial reconciliation sessions, where twenty members from each congregation met over an intense eight-week period. These sessions fostered new partnerships, allowing us to conduct joint community events in both the Afrocentric community on the east side and the predominantly Eurocentric community on the west side. Our collaboration extended internationally, with a joint mission trip to Cape Town and Johannesburg, South Africa, lasting three weeks.

Our "Agenda for Racial Reconciliation" and cross-cultural partnership attracted attention throughout the city and beyond, even capturing the interest of a foundation for racial healing. We conducted workshops for the foundation, and I was appointed as an associate chaplain at the local university, leading to increased attendance from college athletes at our church.

Historic Church Unification and Its Challenges (2002–2004)

Recognizing the momentum in racial reconciliation, the leadership made a historic decision to unite with our suburban partner church, which was part of the same denomination. Together with their pastor and leaders, we collaborated on this union in 2002. My motivations were twofold: to dispel rumors of our church being a cult by joining a longstanding mainline traditional church, and to demonstrate that Christians of different races could worship, serve, and witness together for greater impact. Initially, the relationship seemed promising, but challenges soon emerged.

Despite a strong congregational vote for unification, we observed a decline in attendance between 2002 and 2004. This reflected underlying perceptions and reservations some members held regarding Eurocentric people. Despite these setbacks, my cross-cultural partner and I continued our work within the denomination, participating in urban leadership meetings and promoting racial reconciliation among pastors and churches nationwide.

Facing Judgment and the Decision to Leave

During this period, my previous affair and my commitment to authenticity became points of judgment from church leadership, who appeared to blame me for the decline in attendance. I received a letter and was called to a meeting where I felt admonished and threatened, reminiscent of the spirit that had previously led to my ousting from another denomination.

Meanwhile, my reputation as a reconciler had surfaced in the Carolinas, where my ministry began. I sought guidance through prayer, feeling that God was calling me toward multiethnic church planting, a vision rooted in a four-fold revelation I had received in 1977. I began announcing my intention to transition in ministry, but this announcement was met with silence from the congregation.

My wife was working as a nurse and later joined me on staff as Parish Nurse through the Baptist Hospital, relieving me of some visitation duties and promoting health programs that benefited both the church and the community. Anticipating the move, I encouraged my wife to seek a new job in South Carolina to help bridge the gap in our income. This move also allowed me time to sell our house, which I eventually leased, with an option to buy, to a young couple from the church.

Arranging the Transition

Through a connection made in our urban leadership meetings, I was invited to interview with another church's leadership to plant a multiethnic, cross-cultural church and reach three Afrocentric communities. The interviews were successful, and my hiring was confirmed. I announced my departure from the church in November 2004, and the congregation hosted a going-away fellowship dinner for my wife and me.

Making the Move and Starting Anew

The physical move was challenging, with only two volunteers from the church offering help, and they arrived late. My wife and I, along with the volunteers, loaded a large truck and our cars, enduring muscle spasms in the process. We relocated to a condo in South Carolina and began to settle in.

Once settled, my wife had not yet secured a nursing job, and I was still awaiting confirmation of my salary and starting date from the church's business office, so there was a gap in our finances. I've always walked and moved by faith in what I believed.

Feeling apprehensive, I emailed the man who had recruited me to inquire about the approval. Remarkably, as soon as I clicked send, the letter of approval appeared, officially confirming my new ministry position and salary as Multiethnic Church Planter/Outreach Pastor, beginning in November 2004.

The Launch of a Multiethnic Church Ministry—Relocation and Initial Planning

In 2004, we made a significant transition by moving from our condo in South Carolina to an apartment in North Carolina. With enthusiasm, I quickly began working in my new office, dedicating myself to planning and strategizing ministry efforts aimed at three Afrocentric communities. These efforts also laid the groundwork for planting a multiethnic church. To support this vision, I assembled an urban ministry team and initiated outreach programs targeting both an urban neighborhood and a local refugee community. In addition, I collaborated with the local police department to foster stronger relationships within the community.

Community Engagement and Outreach

Our team organized block parties that drew hundreds of refugees, creating opportunities for connection and engagement. During these events, we met a young Eurocentric man who would later serve as our youth ministry director. Together with church leaders and my team, I traveled across the country to research various models for our ministry. These experiences helped refine our approach and expand our understanding of effective church planting strategies.

Preaching and Core Group Formation

The pastor offered me the valuable opportunity to preach once a month at three different services held on Saturdays and Sundays. This allowed the congregation to experience my preaching style and the depth of my messages. The response was positive, and approximately one hundred people joined me in forming the core group for the multiethnic church.

Racial Reconciliation Sessions

We began meeting weekly over the course of eight weeks, guiding participants through sessions focused on racial reconciliation. These sessions were well received, and the core group eventually narrowed down to about thirty committed participants: 85% Eurocentric, 10% Afrocentric, with the remainder being Latino and Asian.

Establishing Worship Services and Staff

The newly established core group mobilized in a predominantly Afrocentric and Latino community. We began holding worship services at the local YMCA. To support these efforts, we rented office space and expanded the staff to include an administrative assistant and a youth director. Additionally, other volunteers stepped up to serve in various capacities. With these foundational steps in place, our next focus was recruitment.

Recruitment and Worship Growth— Building the Worship Team

To further strengthen our ministry, I reached out to the broader community to recruit individuals for worship roles. Our efforts began with a man from Pennsylvania whom we met during a block party and expanded to include musicians recruited from a local jazz club. Our praise team was formed, consisting of me, my daughters, and other recruited members. Although we welcomed people from diverse backgrounds, each new participant went through an assimilation process, which included affirming their faith in Christ.

Expanding Services and Ministries

Our worship service attendance grew from about thirty people in a smaller room to around ninety in the gymnasium. The number of Afrocentric participants increased, and the youth ministry launched successfully with strong ethnic diversity. In addition, I began recruiting ushers from the adjacent mall, focusing on engaging salespeople. However, as we expanded, we encountered significant challenges that required us to reassess our approach.

XVI. Handwriting on the Wall: A Turning Point in Ministry

Seeking Equity in Church Leadership

As the church congregation grew and more Afrocentric people began attending, I recognized a need for greater equity in leadership. To address this, I advocated for Afrocentric participants to be placed in co-leadership roles alongside ministries and programs that were predominantly led by Eurocentric individuals. My motivation for this change stemmed from scripture, specifically **I Corinthians 3:9**: *"For we are fellow workmen (joint promoters, laborers together) with and for God; you are God's garden and vineyard and field under cultivation, [you are] God's building."*

I was guided not by secular integration but by a spiritual conviction to uphold biblical principles of unity and shared responsibility.

Leadership Conflict and the Inevitable Outcome

After initiating these changes, my leadership was questioned. I met with my recruiter to address the growing allegations about my leadership style, but the meeting did not yield a resolution. It became clear to me that my approach conflicted with the established leadership model of the sponsoring church. I realized that, because the church controlled the finances. They intended to replace me with someone whose leadership style aligned with their own. Eventually, resources were redirected, and participants were encouraged to join a ministry led by an African pastor who was part of my urban ministry team. Again, I felt betrayed!

Resignation and Its Aftermath

My guiding philosophy has always been not to remain where I am unwelcome. Without causing disruption, I submitted my resignation letter. Following this, the principal leaders of the sponsoring church visited my office for a meeting. Rather than seeking a resolution, the meeting focused on reprimanding me. During the discussion, I expressed a willingness to withdraw my resignation, but they declined the offer. With no path to reconciliation, I accepted the situation and prepared to leave.

Again, my philosophy, rooted in scripture, influenced my actions. **Mark 6:11a** states, *"And if any community will not receive and accept and welcome you, and they refuse to listen to you, when you depart, shake off the dust that is on your feet, for a testimony against them..."* I left quietly, packing my belongings and departing without argument.

The next day, Sunday, I delivered my farewell address to the congregation. While some members were emotional and others were puzzled, I refrained from making accusations. To counteract slander and allegations, I relied on the wisdom of **Luke 7:35**: *"Yet wisdom is vindicated (shown to be true and divine) by all her children [by their life, character, and deeds]."* I trusted that, in time, the truth would prevail.

The Emotional Meltdown

On the Monday following my departure, I experienced an emotional breakdown in front of my wife and son in our living room. Overcome with tears, I fell to my knees and cried out to the Lord, "Is your Church real? I'm done with it. You can have it."

The weight of my ministry journey felt like a twelve-round championship fight. In the final round, I was faced with spiritual opposition and relentless accusations that had followed me throughout my ministry. I felt battered by lies, deceit, and deception, and ultimately, I was knocked out and forced out of my ministry role.

Faith, Reflection, and Moving Forward

Although my faith in the church was shaken temporarily, my faith in Christ remained steadfast. I did not view my experience as a mere coincidence or a fatal defeat. Instead, I believed that God was revealing the flaws in my church experience, without suggesting that all churches were the same. I saw this as a divinely orchestrated event under God's providence that would ultimately free me from toxicity and lead me toward a deeper truth that I would come to embrace in the future.

On My Own

After signing a Nondisclosure Agreement and receiving my severance pay and retirement, I found myself, for the first time in my ministry career, without the support of any church organization. This marked a significant turning point where I was truly on my own.

Finding My Sanity

Upon resigning and being released from my position, I experienced a whirlwind of mixed emotions and heightened tension. It felt almost as if I had been gaslighted, leaving me to question whether I was right or wrong in my actions and beliefs. This uncertainty marked the beginning of a new journey—one focused on regaining my sanity. In search of clarity and a way to steady myself, I decided to return to the "real world" and not just confine myself to the church world, and engage with people outside of the church environment. I wanted to understand how those not involved in church would perceive me, hoping their feedback—the so-called "looking glass self"—would help me regain my sense of self-worth and bring me back from the edge.

The Club Scene

Throughout this time, my wife was fully aware of my condition. As a nurse with a compassionate heart and a gift of mercy, she responded with prayerful understanding rather than judgment. She avoided adding to my emotional turmoil with criticism or arguments, choosing instead to offer support and gentle admonition. She encouraged me to be careful, and for this, I affectionately call her my Sarah. Even in moments of disagreement, she remained supportive and redemptive.

Seeking a new environment, I began frequenting a sophisticated club scene known for attracting mature adults. During these outings, I encountered a variety of people, including politicians, businesspeople, and, surprisingly, some church members and a youth minister. I openly shared my story, framing it within the context of my faith journey. Rather than meeting me with rejection or criticism, these individuals responded with acceptance and understanding, providing the positive feedback I desperately needed during this transitional period.

A Strange Visitation—An Unfamiliar Place

A period of silence and doubt:

For a year and a half, I chose not to attend any church. During this period, I felt no indication that God was speaking to my heart. My conscience did not trouble me or convict me about my actions, leading me to continue on the same path, and I reasoned that I wasn't doing anything wrong. The conscience can be a peculiar place to navigate. Even though I maintained my faith in the Lord, the absence of His voice in my conscience brought back feelings of abandonment, reminiscent of my experiences with my father. I began to question whether the Father of fathers had abandoned me, or if perhaps my faith was misaligned.

A Breakthrough in Faith

Eventually, I experienced a breakthrough in my faith through an unusual circumstance. This event shattered the theological limitations that had previously hindered me, propelling my faith to a new spiritual level described in the parables throughout Scripture. My renewed faith became centered solely on God's sacred written Word, leaving behind any theological or doctrinal preferences.

The Unusual Encounter

The beginning of this transformation occurred just as those eighteen months of silence were coming to an end. I had a strange experience at a gentlemen's club. Before sharing the details, I'm reminded of **Hebrews 13:2**: *"Do not forget or neglect or refuse to extend hospitality to strangers [in the brotherhood---being friendly, cordial, and gracious, sharing the comforts of your home and doing your part generously], for through it some have entertained angels without knowing it."* Just as spiritual gifts are real, so too is the possibility of angelic visits, though recognizing them requires faith in the unknown being revealed.

It was 2009, and I was feeling depressed and lonely at home, having resigned from the ministry eighteen months prior. I called my nephew and asked if I could come spend time with him. He agreed, and after I arrived, we decided to visit a gentlemen's club together.

We arrived in the late afternoon, just before evening. The club was nearly empty. I sat at the bar and ordered a drink, while my nephew took a seat by the stage. A dancer approached and sat in front of me at the bar, using suggestive body language. Yet my thoughts were elsewhere—I was preoccupied with the feeling that I had disappointed the Lord by leaving the ministry. Sensing something was wrong, she asked me about it, but I replied that nothing was the matter.

At that moment, another dancer seated on the opposite side of the bar beckoned me over. I moved to where she sat and took a seat next to her. She appeared older than most dancers, though not truly old. She spoke to me directly and without hesitation: **"I see your light. Your church will not understand you, but you need to go back to what God called you to."** Her words stunned me. If someone from the church had said this, I might not have believed them.

Immediately, I returned to my nephew and told him we needed to leave. After dropping him off, I got on the interstate and called my wife. I stated, "You won't believe this, but…" She stopped me and said, "Come on home, baby, and we'll see what the Lord will do." Within two weeks, I was back in ministry.

A Divided Heart

Two weeks after my experience at the gentlemen's club, God opened a door for my return to ministry. However, I found myself living with one foot in the church and one foot still in the club. The truth was that I enjoyed the club scene and the respect and attention I received there—people saw me as a successful man and affectionately called me "Hollywood."

XVII. My Second Multiethnic Church Plant

After relocating to a new area and purchasing a home, I was recruited to serve on staff at another predominantly Eurocentric church located just down the road. I developed a strong friendship with the pastor, who, like me, was deeply interested in the work of racial reconciliation. My official role was associate pastor of neighborhood outreach, serving a diverse community similar to that of my previous church.

To prepare for ministry, I first completed an internship and then began the important task of identifying the most suitable location for planting a new multiethnic church. Yet, during this time, I found myself struggling with a sense of belonging. I felt as though I existed in two worlds: one within the church, where I often felt uncomfortable while preaching or serving communion, and another in the clubs, where my presence was more familiar. I also felt out of place at many denominational events and activities, frequently feeling invisible and avoided by others. Despite these challenges, I remained committed to my calling.

Building Community and Establishing the Church

Relying on my gift of Apostleship and my understanding of demographic trends, I identified a gentrifying neighborhood as an ideal site for a new multiethnic congregation. While building relationships in the community, I befriended a successful local businessman who owned a popular restaurant. We began holding Bible study sessions at his establishment, which quickly grew to about thirty participants representing various ethnic backgrounds. As our numbers increased, we started searching for a permanent church facility and eventually found one in the same location as the restaurant. Renovations soon followed.

Church Launch and Growth

That summer, we officially launched the church with approximately fifty people in attendance. The initial momentum was strong, and the church continued to grow. However, as we began to focus more intentionally on racial reconciliation, I encountered the same difficulties that had arisen at my previous multiethnic church.

Transition to Academia

Ultimately, these recurring challenges led to my resignation. Shortly thereafter, I was offered and accepted an adjunct professorship at a local college and seminary. Around 2012, I began teaching as an Adjunct Professor of Urban Studies. Still, I found myself divided, maintaining my role in the church while also remaining active in the club scene, where I had become quite popular.

Deliverance through Circumstances

Based on the experiences detailed in this book, I have come to understand that God's method of delivering His people generally occurs in two main ways: **First,** God delivers individuals from adverse and toxic environments and relationships by dramatically disrupting their situations. This disruption can be compared to the "dunamis" or dynamite witness power referenced in **Acts 1:8**, which forcefully breaks apart the circumstances that caused distress and removes toxic individuals from their lives. **Secondly**, once these negative situations have been dismantled, the individual then enters a process of spiritual cleansing, which is similar to the **"Breaking the Yoke"** described earlier in the text.

Furthermore, I have realized that God often works most powerfully in silence. Even during times when it seems that God is not speaking, He is quietly working behind the scenes. This is comparable to the construction of the first temple, as described in **I Kings 6:7**, where Solomon was instructed to prepare the stones at the quarry so that no sound of hammer, chisel, or iron tools would be heard during the building of the temple. This practice highlighted the sacredness of the project. In the same way, our bodies are described as the temple of the Holy Spirit in **I Corinthians 6:19-20.** God works internally, away from the noise and distractions of the world, creating a peaceful and sacred environment within us that is centered on Christ.

In this silent work, I came to realize that God had not abandoned me but was doing a greater work by allowing me the space to reach an epiphany and to open my spiritual eyes, leading to deeper understanding and growth.

Feelings of Betrayal—The Jonah Experience

During this period, I found myself feeling what I call a "Jonah experience." Like Jonah, who fled from his divine calling as described in **Jonah 1:3**, I was also running from my own calling. My reasons stemmed from a growing dislike for church people and a sense of betrayal. Jonah's reluctance was based on his disdain for the Ninevites, an ancient Assyrian people who had long oppressed Israel. Although Jonah was aware that God would forgive them if they repented, in his humanity, he preferred that they face judgment instead.

Similarly, I felt betrayed and abandoned by the church, believing that I had been blackballed and blacklisted. This experience led me to want nothing more to do with the church, echoing Jonah's conflict and resistance to his calling.

The Accumulation of Resignations & Their Effects

Throughout my professional and spiritual journey, I have always maintained a principle: I reiterate, I do not remain in places where I am not wanted, nor do I cause unnecessary disturbance. This approach has allowed me to leave organizations on amicable terms, ensuring that no previous employer or church authority can claim that I was dismissed or departed due to animosity. My departures have never been dictated by unfavorable circumstances; rather, I believe that God guides and delivers us from such situations.

Elijah's Syndrome: A Guiding Principle

I also likened my experience to what I call **"Elijah's Syndrome,"** drawing inspiration from the story found in **I Kings, chapter 19**.

After achieving a miraculous victory over 450 false prophets of Baal, Elijah's life was threatened by Jezebel. In response, and out of apprehension for his life, he ran away, journeying for forty days, sustained by the Lord's strength and provisions, until he reached Horeb, the mountain of God, and hid in a cave. There, the presence of God passed by, and He invited Elijah to behold the backside of His glory. God then presented Elijah with a test—a powerful wind, an earthquake, and a fire—but revealed that He was not in any of these dramatic manifestations. Instead, God spoke through a still small voice, teaching Elijah that true guidance comes from within rather than from external circumstances.

In my own life, I strive to follow this principle. I do not allow circumstances to dictate my decisions; instead, I listen for God's internal guidance, seeking His direction above all else.

A Clean Record of Departure

My record remains untarnished when it comes to leaving organizations. I am committed to leaving each place better than I found it, making a positive impact before my departure. Over the years, I have resigned from four church organizations, as well as from my position as an adjunct professor.

Transition to New Chapters

Here, I recount my resignation from my second multiethnic church, which preceded my decision to step down from my adjunct professorship. These transitions mark significant moments in my journey, each shaped by a commitment to integrity, spiritual guidance, and purposeful closure.

Around 2012, I made the difficult decision to resign from my second multiethnic church plant. After stepping away from pastoral ministry, I transitioned into a new role as an adjunct professor at a local Christian college and seminary. This opportunity was profoundly uplifting; I felt as though I was being fully restored to ministry. My primary responsibility was to teach preachers and students who aspired to serve in various capacities within ministry. The years I spent pastoring became a valuable source of information, and the extensive materials I had developed over time formed the foundation for the curriculum I created.

My classes were well-received, and I became popular among the students. They seemed to genuinely enjoy my approach to teaching.

Notably, the majority of the student body was Afrocentric, while most of the professors were Eurocentric Evangelicals. This dynamic created some tension, as several professors appeared to have issues with the content and perspectives I brought into the classroom.

Another Crisis

After a particularly difficult time related to a gentlemen's club experience, I decided to recommit myself to serving the Lord—whether or not I was officially in ministry. I left the club scene behind and concentrated on fulfilling the vision God revealed to me in 1977.

One pivotal night, I dropped a young man off at his mother's house after sharing my faith with him. He was considering converting to Islam. After dropping him off and before heading home, I stopped for a few beers, having three twelve-ounce glasses in total before leaving.

As I prepared to drive home, I initially considered taking the long way but ultimately chose the shorter route. I called my wife to let her know I was on my way home. However, when I turned onto the street leading to my house, I encountered a police sobriety checkpoint. I remained calm, confident that I was not intoxicated. At the checkpoint, a police officer stopped me, shone a flashlight across my face and the passenger side, and noticed a half pint of gin left by the young man I had been mentoring. The officer explained that he had not intended to have me step out for a sobriety check since my eyes were not glassy and my breath did not smell of alcohol, but the presence of the open container changed his mind.

My **third** assessment of God delivering us is based on our right decisions. We can't blame everything we do on the devil. What we do, regardless of our influence, is a choice. I've learned since then that our indecision and mistakes can lead us in the wrong direction; consequently, we must be aware of people and circumstances **(Ephesians 5:15-17)**.

Anxious about the potential consequences for my family and my position at the school, I stepped out of the car. My nervousness caused me to fail the walk-the-line test. I was then taken to a trailer where, after several attempts, I finally registered a 0.08 on the breathalyzer—the legal limit in North Carolina. Despite this, I was arrested, my car was impounded, and I was taken to the station for booking. I called my wife to inform her of the situation. Later that morning, after being released, the young man I had mentored picked me up and helped me recover my car.

To my surprise, both the school and the denomination responded with grace upon learning about the incident. When I went to court, the police officer claimed that my breathalyzer reading was 1.00, a statement I knew was untrue. Unfortunately, my public defender did not request evidence to contest this claim. I believed I was a victim of racial profiling. The judge dismissed the open container charge and expressed belief in my account, but still found me guilty of DUI. As a result, I was restricted from driving after 9:00 PM, required to attend eight weeks of DUI instruction, and assigned community service, during which I shared my faith with others.

Through these challenges, I chose not to blame anyone for my difficulties. Instead, I viewed these experiences as a form of "reaping and sowing" and continued my work at the college. However, after that incident, I became more uncomfortable with my role as a professor because of the growing political tension in the country and how evangelicals were aligning with politics, pushing a conservative agenda that seemed to be opposed to ethnic minorities, which was "a" focus of my calling, so I resigned around 2016 and moved on.

XVIII. Reflections on Evangelicalism and My Journey

From the beginning of my involvement in evangelism, I was closely associated with evangelicals. At that time, I saw no distinction between evangelism and evangelicalism—both were centered solely on reaching the lost for Christ and engaging in discipleship. This perspective shaped much of my early ministry work and approach to church leadership.

Political Shifts in Evangelicalism

However, in 2016, I witnessed a significant transformation within the evangelical movement as political evangelicalism began to rise. This shift was particularly evident in the denomination that I led our urban church to join in 2004, which identified as evangelical. Additionally, both denominations in which I planted multiethnic churches were considered evangelical. Yet, by 2016, it became apparent that evangelicalism was becoming more politicized, and in some instances, there was even support for extremism.

Questioning Motives and Theological Underpinnings

This political turn prompted me to reflect on my earlier motivations for planting multiethnic churches. I began to wonder if the underlying drive for these efforts was, in fact, to assimilate ethnic minorities into the prevailing political and social perspectives held by evangelicals. This notion seems to stem from their theological stance on the Millennium, particularly the post-millennialist view.

Among the four main theories regarding the thousand-year reign of Christ, post-millennialists maintain that Christ will govern from the heavenly throne through the Church on earth, establishing a theocracy alongside the Government during this era, before His eventual return. Aligned with this concept is their cultural view of Christ as a Nationalist Messiah, justifying it from such scripture as **Psalms 33:12**, ***"Blessed (happy, fortunate, to be envied) is the nation whose God is the Lord, the people He has chosen as His heritage."*** During this period, their focus would be exclusively on their interpretation of the gospel, without regard for issues of human justice, equality, or human rights.

Personal Resolution and Departure

Arriving at these conclusions led to questioning from some professors and the Dean concerning my beliefs. As a result, I made the decision to resign. Throughout this process, I have maintained a non-partisan stance regarding politics, choosing not to align with the left, right, or any position in between. Instead, I continue to vote according to my conscience.

—The Racial Barrier—Walls of Partition—

Reflecting on my experiences, I do not interpret my departure from two Eurocentric churches as an act of discrimination. While there were evident racial prejudices—something present across all ethnicities and cultures—these tended to manifest as xenophobia: a discomfort or unfamiliarity with those of different backgrounds. It is important to distinguish between xenophobia and racial prejudice. Racial prejudice exists universally, ranging from passive forms that all people possess to moderate forms where individuals avoid those of other races, and even to extreme prejudice, which is characterized by hatred toward those not of one's own race.

Extreme racial prejudice aligns with racism, a concept I believe was historically constructed for economic advantage, particularly over people of darker skin tones. This mindset was perpetuated through generations, serving collective economic interests. At its core, extreme racial prejudice is driven by a desire to control the economy and dominate ethnic minorities, with certain groups claiming superiority as a means to justify this control.

Biblical Perspective on Race and Ethnicity

Interestingly, the terms "race" and "racial" do not appear in the Bible. Instead, Scripture refers to "nations," derived from the word "Ethnos," and "ethnicities," which relate to family heritage and lineage. Humanity has evolved from different family lines, adapting to diverse cultures as a means of survival. **Genesis 11** recounts the migrations of Shem, Ham, and Japheth, who settled in distinct regions and developed unique cultures—as city dwellers, seafarers, and nomadic farmers. The latter, eventually becoming God's covenant people.

The Hope of Unity

Ultimately, as believers redeemed by the Lord, we have the promise of living together in New Jerusalem, united in faith and immortality. The vision described in **Revelation 7:9a** captures this future: *"After this I looked* *and a vast host appeared which no one could count, [gathered out] of every nation, from all tribes and peoples and languages..."* Until that glorious fulfillment, the gospel remains the source of power capable of breaking down racial barriers between people; that is a heart condition, and the heart (Man's Conscience) can only be broken by the power of God's Spirit, through the Gospel.

Political legislation draws outward lines through law to prevent racial hate, but only the gospel can change the heart. This conviction fueled my ministry of racial reconciliation **(II Corinthians 5:16-21)** and may explain why it faced spiritual resistance. I believe this resistance is spiritual, for Satan—the "prince of the power of the air" and "god of this world"—recognizes that unity among God's diverse people signals the imminent end of his influence, as his strategy has always been to divide and conquer those called to reach God's harvest.

Conflict of Ministry Models

What some interpret as racial prejudice in the church, I see as a conflict between ministry models, values, and cultural norms. The approach I adopted was a justice empowerment model that aims to assist community members with job placement, home ownership, education, higher education, and business start-ups. In contrast, the traditional model employed by the sponsoring churches focused on charity and mercy, organizing projects for volunteers to serve those deemed "least and lost." For these churches, the benefit was a transition from personal success to significance, providing a basis for relationships with Afrocentric people. Yet, underlying these models is a historical barrier that can only be overcome by the "power of the gospel" **(Romans 1:16)**.

Authentic Christianity and Racial Prejudice

Racism and racial prejudice have no place within Christian circles—specifically, within the Body of Christ, which comprises God's called-out people **(Ecclesia)** from around the world. Christianity is not confined to institutions or any specific country with specific theological or doctrinal preferences. It is culturally neutral, emphasizing kingdom principles and righteous living. If racial prejudice is present, it is not authentic Christianity but rather a culturally adapted version.

As God's anointed and diverse people, our mission is to dismantle the barriers, or strongholds, that separate us. **Ephesians 2:13-15** affirms this calling:

But now in Christ Jesus, you who once were [so] far away, through (by, in) the blood of Christ have been brought near.

For He is [Himself] our peace (our bond of unity and harmony). He has made us both [Jew and Gentile] one [body], and has broken down (destroyed, abolished) the hostile dividing wall between us,

By abolishing in His [own crucified] flesh the enmity [caused by] the Law with its decrees and ordinances [which He annulled]; that He from the two might create in Himself one new man

[one new quality of humanity out of the two], so making peace.

Stage III: Wounded Healers in Action—Brokenness made Whole

XIX. The Meaning of Unorthodox

Understanding Unorthodox Christianity

This is the third stage that completes the pathway to wholeness.

The term "orthodox" has a historical and theological significance that dates back to the formative years of the Christian faith, approximately between AD 150 and 725. During this era, the Church Fathers, who were also known as Bishops, diligently established the essential beliefs that defined Christianity. Their primary focus was on clarifying doctrines such as the Trinity and Christology—the understanding of Christ's nature and his role within the faith. Etymologically, the word "orthodox" refers to the faith of the majority, specifically those who contributed to shaping these foundational beliefs.

Divergence from Orthodoxy

Over time, various movements within the church led to new interpretations and departures from established orthodoxies, particularly in areas like Soteriology, which deals with the doctrine of salvation. As a result, a minority of churches and believers began to embrace distinct perspectives regarding the essentials of faith necessary for salvation. My own faithful journey aligns with this minority perspective, which I describe as unorthodox. I do not adhere to all the specific distinctions about what defines a Christian according to orthodox teachings, as I believe they are not all required for salvation.

Core Beliefs of Unorthodox Faith

John Wesley, a prominent Reformer, once remarked, **"If it doesn't strike against the root of Christianity,**

I think and let think." Guided by this principle, my unorthodox Christian faith centers on the essentials required for salvation:

- Belief that Christ existed from all eternity as the Lord of glory.
- Affirmation of His birth to the virgin Mary, manifesting God in the flesh.
- Acceptance of His public ministry and miracles as prophesied evidence of His Messiahship.
- Recognition of His crucifixion as a sacrifice for the sins of the world.
- Belief in His resurrection to immortal life, providing the foundation for our eternal life and resurrection.
- Understanding of His ascension back to glory, where He took His throne as the Lord of glory.
- Receiving the Promise of the Spirit, which descended upon and indwelt the disciples and established the Early Church.

According to **Romans 10:9-13**, salvation comes when we believe in the revealed Lord with our heart and confess with our mouth. These statements are encapsulated in the Apostles' Creed, and I maintain that nothing beyond this is needed for salvation.

Unorthodox Teachings of Christ

Christ's teachings themselves were considered unorthodox when compared to orthodox Judaism.

Unlike the religious leaders of His time, Jesus spoke with inherent authority and did not rely on quoting Rabbis to validate His teachings. This distinction is captured in **Matthew 7:28-29**:

When Jesus had finished these sayings [the Sermon on the Mount], the crowds were astonished and overwhelmed with bewildered wonder at His Teachings,

For He was teaching as One Who had [and was] authority, and not as [did] the scribes.

Jesus did not depend on others to affirm the truth of God, setting His approach apart from traditional teachings.

As a consequence of Christ's unorthodox style, He was known as a friend to sinners, misunderstood by the religious establishment, and criticized as the prince of devils, Beelzebub **(Matthew 12:24)**. So, it is not unusual for the followers of Christ to be criticized the same way. *"If the world hates you, know that it hated Me before it hated you. If you belonged to the world, the world would treat you with affection and would love you as its own. But because you are not of the world [no longer one with it], but I have chosen (selected) you out of the world, the world hates (detests) you"* (**John 15:18-19**). Consider, if you will, that churches can have worldly elements.

Similarly, I faced stereotypes and criticism for engaging with people outside the church's walls, reflecting God's outreach beyond institutional boundaries.

The Foundation of Salvation

Unorthodoxy is likened to left-handed athletes achieving results differently. The means—faith and grace—justify the end, which is eternal salvation. The assurance of life after death is the ultimate goal of salvation. Saving faith brings certainty, not anxiety or fear over life's end or Christ's return. It assures believers that their salvation is secure, and death is but a passage into bliss.

The essential truth I uphold is the Lord's prescription for salvation: faith as a divine gift, repentance, and confession that Yeshua (Jesus) is Lord, coupled with an unwavering belief in the "verity" of God's inspired Word. Although these convictions may be viewed as unorthodox, they do not cross into heresy. On the contrary, I am more committed than ever to the fundamental essentials of faith.

—My Pragmatic Approach to Scripture—

The simplicity of theology can be understood as "man's concept of God," seen from different vantage points of the human experience. People come to their conclusions about God in one of two primary ways. **First**, through the lens of Theism's **Transcendence**, God is seen as existing above, over, and beyond human comprehension. In this view, understanding God requires a deliberate, step-by-step process—known as liturgy—using a theological framework to study and comprehend Him. **Second**, the **Immanence** of God describes God as being immediately present in a person's life and circumstances. The reality is that, in His omnipresence, God is both transcendent and immanent. The sole lens through which these truths can be recognized is Scripture alone.

The Principle of Scriptural Interpretation

A well-known adage coined by a scholastic theologian state, **"If Scripture sense makes common sense, seek no other sense."** This saying captures the essence of my approach to interpreting Scripture. I adhere to the belief that if the plain reading of Scripture makes sense, there is no need to search for additional meanings. This is aside from fundamentalism, which interprets Scripture from translation surfaces, while plain truth delves below the surface of translations. Because of this, my teachings may sometimes be perceived as unorthodox, especially by those who are accustomed to traditional or orthodox interpretations. My perspective is shaped by a straightforward approach to the meaning of Scripture.

Pragmatism in Teaching God's Word

In the context of communicating God's Word, my understanding of pragmatism is rooted in practicality and accessibility. I strive to make theological concepts understandable and relevant to the common person. My method begins with individuals who may have little or no formal education and extends to those with advanced education.

I align my concept with the thoughts of a respected theologian who noted, **"All false systems of theology begin with man and seek to work up to God. In all our thinking, we must begin with God and**

work down to man." Guided by this principle, I start with the higher truths found in the original languages of Scripture and then bring their meaning down to everyday life. My goal is to make these truths accessible and practical in the real world—where people live, work, play, and in interactions where spiritual discussions are grounded in daily experience, known as the God-talk.

To achieve this, I intentionally avoid using church jargon, clichés, or complex doctrinal terms. Instead, I communicate in plain language that resonates with everyone, whether they are believers (the regenerate) or nonbelievers (the unregenerate). This approach ensures that the message is meaningful and relatable to all.

XX. New Ministry Approach— Journey Toward Harmony and Unity

Higher Truth Concepts: Addressing Suppressed Issues

My previous approaches are rooted in higher truth concepts, which I call **Kingdom Concepts**, that are designed to resolve and reconcile suppressed issues within families and churches. These methods aim to help individuals and groups unload the burdens and baggage of the past, working purposefully toward **harmony in relationships** and **unity of purpose**.

Answering the Call: Continuing the Ministry Journey

After resigning from my professorship in 2016, I felt a profound conviction that my ministry journey was far from over. The sense that I should not abandon my calling was reinforced by the words of **I Corinthians 9:16-17**: *"For if I [merely] preach the Gospel, that gives me no reason to boast, for I feel compelled of necessity to do it. Woe is me if I do not preach the glad tidings (the Gospel)!*

For if I do this work of my own free will, then I have my pay (my reward); but if it is not of my own will, but is done reluctantly and under compulsion, I am [still] entrusted with a [sacred] trusteeship and commission."

These verses strengthened my resolve to continue preaching, regardless of personal circumstances.

Prophetic Preparation and Spiritual Insight

Reflecting on **II Kings 6:8-20**, I recall how the prophet Elisha was warned about the Syrian king's ambush. In a similar spiritual sense, each time I resigned from a position, the Lord provided insight into what was to come. This was true during my professorship as well. While still serving before 2016, I began anticipating my eventual resignation and immersed myself in prayerful research for the next chapter of my ministry.

Evolving Preaching Style: Inspiration and Scriptural Depth

During this period, I contemplated adopting a pragmatic and unorthodox preaching style, while I recognized that some might perceive this as adding to established Scripture. However, I intended to draw deeper inspiration from the Spirit, exploring the original languages of Scripture without altering or diminishing its message. Despite these concerns, I was convinced that my ministry required a suitable platform to share this evolved approach.

Seeking a New Platform for Ministry

Between 2014 and 2016, I wrote an article on Predictive Prophecy titled **"The Shift,"** which I presented to professors and students at the college. This article marked an important milestone in my search for a new platform to share my ministry and the pragmatic style I had developed.

"The Shift" highlighted passages such as **Daniel 12:4**, which speaks of knowledge increasing and people moving "to and fro." I compared this to **Genesis 6**, referencing the boundless imagination, and **Genesis 11:4**, where the builders under Nimrod aspired to construct a tower to heaven. While the ancient technology behind such feats remains a matter of debate, **Genesis 11:6** reveals that God intervened because nothing would be withheld from the people's imagination. I noted that ancient technology was closely tied to nature, as seen in excavations of civilizations like the Egyptian Pyramids.

I drew connections between these teachings and the internet generation during prophetic times, suggesting that the turn of the century in 2000 would see an influx of evil spiritual forces, described as coming from the **"prince of the power of the air"**—interpreted as air waves spreading lies and conspiracy theories. This, I argued, would stem from the **"spirit of antichrist."** I also emphasized that God was providing new marching orders for the Church to establish a presence on the internet to pragmatically address social media and emerging podcasters and influencers, combating their information with higher truth. Although "The Shift" was met with smiles and laughter, it did not deter me from launching my internet ministry platform.

Building Online Ministry Platforms

During this time, my initial effort was to organize a **Virtual Church** online, titled **Church in the Middle**. After starting with home meetings for a small group, I decided it was not the right time and discontinued the effort. My next initiative was to create an editing and self-publishing service, **JJ Planter Editing & Self-Publishing**, aimed at "**Getting the Word Out**" through a dedicated website. I also shared my writings on social media. This platform continued until 2021, resulting in the release of about 30 client books and four of my own. The workload became overwhelming without staff support, leading me to dissolve the service and establish a smaller, more focused offering: **JJ Planter Writing & Ministry Consulting**. This service remains active today, with an even greater emphasis on online ministry.

Middle Mission: Expanding the Vision

In collaboration with a few others, I developed Middle Mission, an outgrowth of Church in the Middle. The focus is on forming small home mission groups networked together, emphasizing economic development, group cohesiveness, and community outreach. Today, we continue to build the platform, focusing our efforts on evangelism and discipleship, both locally and internationally. **The immediate focus is on fostering harmony in relationships and unity of purpose in families and among churches.**

Refined Through Trials as a Mission Developer

Before I could fully embrace this new direction and my new identity as a Mission Developer, I had to endure a series of trials that I've shared in this book. These experiences tested my character, broadened my perspective, and ultimately shaped both my ministry approach and my commitment to serving others. Through these refining moments, I found a renewed sense of purpose and dedication to my calling, which continues to guide me in my journey of faith and service.

Refocusing

Over the years, my commitment to my calling deepened, and I became known as the **"People's Pastor,"** performing weddings, conducting funerals, consulting with mission/ministry development, and occasionally public speaking. My focus shifted from not only serving traditional church members to reaching out to those outside the conventional church community. This shift has led to an intentional effort to create the Outpost Community Ministry, which is still in the planning stages. Eventually, it can become small church plants that provide a spiritual home for individuals who may not have felt welcome in a traditional church setting.

The New Focus

Imagine a scenario of 100 people in a church setting versus thousands of people connecting online, considering the value of worship experiences and preaching. Now, do a statistical assessment of each setting. Also, consider the effects of millions of followers of podcasters and influencers and how their thinking is shaped.

In my experience at the Afrocentric church, I observed people growing spiritually, and I still receive testimonies about their lives today. They are not your typical churchgoers, but they have found their way in the real world as normal people following Christ. On the other hand, I have often heard from other churchgoers about their worship experience. Most didn't remember the title of the sermon or what it was exactly about, but they responded that it sounded good. In my Eurocentric Church experience and ministry, the truth that I shared was weighed in the balance with uncertainty and met with skepticism. On the other hand, I receive hundreds and thousands of "likes" and "loves" and positive comments about my posts online. I know that fellowship matters, but aside from the fellowship, who do you think benefits most from the message? Now, on to the meat of this concluding stage:

XXI. Building Harmony of Relationship & Unity of Purpose

The title is taken from **Matthew 18:18-20**, which our Lord extracts from how elders (Aldermen) governed the ancient cities of Israel when they met at the city gates. Meeting at the gates was symbolic of the keys that control what goes into the city and what doesn't. Their method of decision-making was founded upon complete, unanimous agreement—never on the notion of agreeing to disagree. If they could not resolve an issue for the city, they would table the meeting and reconvene when they were all in agreement. In context, Christ was saying that if leaders in the church came into 100% agreement on the "Cause of Christ," He would make it happen on earth from heaven. Likewise, if they didn't agree, it would not happen. (I've seen both throughout my ministry).

The Principle of Unanimity

The tone of the passage resembles a musical composition, where harmony and unity are essential. Like a master conductor (Christ) leading an orchestra, He blends diverse instruments to create perfect harmony. This harmony is born out of a shared purpose—the cause of Christ—extracted from the promise that "two or three gathered in His name" accomplish His will.

This section introduces the Kingdom Concept, which is further explored in the rest of the book up to the conclusion. It focuses on the idea that true unity and harmony come from aligning with Christ's purpose and working together for His cause.

—Introducing the Kingdom Concept of Wounded Healers—

The idea of "Wounded Healers" is rooted in the prophetic words of **Isaiah 53:5**: *"But He was wounded for our transgressions, He was bruised for our guilt and iniquities; the chastisement [needful to obtain] peace and well-being for us was upon Him, and with the stripes [that wounded] Him we are healed and made whole."*

While some interpret this verse as a promise of physical healing based on the philosophy of metaphysics rooted in the prosperity gospel, its deeper meaning is about becoming whole in our humanity through Christ's redemptive work on the cross. True healing is not merely physical but spiritual, restoring our relationship with God and making us whole persons in Christ.

The Spirituality & Unity of Wounded Healers

Unity among believers is not about outward sameness or uniformity. Instead, it is an inward kinship rooted in Christ and our shared spiritual heritage. To understand unity, we must first clarify what being spiritual isn't:

- **Being spiritual is not spiritism.** It is not about following universal laws or mystical principles that guide life apart from God.
- **Being spiritual is not legalism.** It is not about rigidly following religious rules to achieve a sinless standard.
- **Being spiritual is not asceticism.** It is not about strict self-denial from worldly pleasures to attain a higher spiritual goal by mortifying the flesh.

Being spiritual is about living a normal, natural life because there is no separation scripturally between the sacred and the secular. Spiritual believers live a normal, natural life following the dictates of the moral law, written on the tablet of their heart, within their God-consciousness. That walk of faith in scripture is described as being "led of the Spirit." Therefore, being spiritual is about discipleship, following the ways of the Lord in the real world, growing into Christlike character.

The biblical concept of sin, whether in Hebrew **("chata'ah")** or Greek **("hamartia")**, means **"to miss the mark,"** or to fail to obey God's revealed will to the human conscience. This imagery comes from archery: missing the target entirely.

In the Genesis narrative, Adam's disobedience was not just a personal failure but a fall for all humanity, as he genetically represented the entire human race. As a result, every person inherits a tendency within human nature to disobey God's moral law—a law written on the conscience. The moral conscience is the still small voice of God embedded in the soul as the breath of God from creation, which gives humanity the innate awareness of right and wrong. **Romans 2:14-15:**

When Gentiles who have not the [divine] Law do instinctively what the Law requires, they are a law to themselves, since they do not have the Law.

They show that the essential requirements of the Law are written in their hearts *and* **are operating there, with which their consciences (sense of right and wrong) also bear witness; and their [moral] decisions (their arguments of reason, their condemning or approving thoughts) will accuse or perhaps defend** *and* **excuse [them].**

When the first man, representing humanity, violated God's command in the garden, spiritual death preceded physical death. Spiritual death happened instantaneously, resulting in the God-consciousness, the human spirit, being alienated from God and suppressed within his soul, the self-consciousness. His God-consciousness no longer dominated his being. Instead, his self-consciousness, the seat of his will, subject to good and evil, intellect, emotions, lust, passions, and selfishness, governed his life. That is the legacy of the fall of man. **Psalms 51:5,** *"Behold, I was brought forth in [a state of] iniquity; my mother was sinful who conceived me [and I too am sinful]."*

Romans 5:12 explains: *"Therefore, as sin came into the world through one man, and death as the result of sin, so death spread to all men, [no* *one being able to stop it or to escape its power] because all men sinned."* This inherited condition is what the Bible refers to as the *"law of sin and death"* **(Romans 8:2)**.

The Good News of Redemption

When a person experiences the new birth, commonly called "being born again," the human spirit, or God-consciousness, is delivered from suppression in the soul and indwelt by the Spirit of God, giving them new life that empowers them to overcome a sinful lifestyle ruled by self-consciousness. Just as natural birth is an unimaginable miracle that is profiled scientifically and medically, so is spiritual birth an unexplainable miracle profiled in Scripture as conception by the Spirit of God. **I Peter 1:23,** *"You have been regenerated (born again), not from a mortal origin (seed, sperm), but from one that is immortal by the ever living and lasting Word of God."* **I John 3:9,** *"No one born (begotten) of God [deliberately, knowingly, and habitually] practices sin, for God's nature abides in him [His principle of life, the divine sperm, remains permanently within him]; and he cannot practice sinning because he is born (begotten) of God."*

The message of the Gospel is one of hope and transformation. **Romans 8:1-2** declares: *"Therefore, [there is] now no condemnation (no adjudging guilty of wrong) for those who are in Christ Jesus, who live [and] walk not after the dictates of the flesh, but after the dictates of the Spirit. For the law of the Spirit of life [which is] in Christ Jesus [the law of our new being] has freed me from the law of sin and of death."*

Through Christ's sacrifice, believers are set free from the power of sin and death. The journey of faith begins with this new birth, but believers still wrestle with the **"old man"**—the remnants of their former nature.

The Journey of a Wounded Healer

Wounded healers are believers who have faced and overcome the burdens of their past. Though they still have flaws and weaknesses, these do not define them. Unfortunately, religious communities often judge these imperfections harshly. However, the truth remains that all in Christ has been declared righteous through God's judicial justification:

"For our sake He made Christ [virtually] to be sin Who knew no sin, so that in and through Him we might become [endued with, viewed as being in, and examples of] the righteousness of God [what we ought to be, approved and acceptable and in right relationship with Him, by His goodness]" **(II Corinthians 5:21).**

Believers are called to ignore criticism and continue pursuing God's purpose—reaching out to others with compassion. Wounded healers, or any Christian for that matter, never reach perfection in this life, but they grow in love. As **I John 4:18** says: *"There is no fear in love [dread does not exist], but full-grown (complete, perfect) love turns fear out of doors and expels every trace of terror! For fear brings with it the thought of punishment, and [so] he who is afraid has not reached the full maturity of love [is not yet grown into love's complete perfection]."*

Apprehensions and worries about sin impede growth in love. It is love that perfects wholeness and maturity in believers. Their experiences of brokenness make them more empathetic, allowing them to help others who struggle with similar issues. Their past does not define them, but it equips them to minister to others.

Wounded Healers Understand the Nature of Sin

The doctrine of original sin is often misunderstood as labeling people as inherently bad or condemned. In reality, it describes the universal human condition—our tendency to miss the mark and violate God's revealed will. This understanding helps wounded healers relate to others with humility and grace, recognizing that everyone shares similar struggles. *"Be well balanced (temperate, sober of mind), be vigilant and cautious at all times; for that enemy of yours, the devil, roams around like a lion roaring [in fierce hunger], seeking someone to seize upon and devour.*

Withstand him; be firm in faith [against his onset—rooted, established, strong, immovable, and determined], knowing that the same (identical) sufferings are appointed to your brotherhood (the whole body of Christians) throughout the world" **(I Peter 5:8-9).**

Wounded Healers Mending Relationships

In earlier discussions, we explored the forces that divide families, communities, and churches. Now, we focus on how wounded healers can foster **harmony in relationships** and **unity of purpose**.

True believers often struggle with feelings of unworthiness, guilt, and shame, especially when hurt by others within the church. **Wounded healers mending relationships** are about serving others through their pain, finding healing for themselves and those they help. But it's not like someone with an addiction trying to help someone else with the same addiction. That only compounds the problem. It's more like the wounded healer reflects on and remembers that they had the same problems but overcame them.

To move forward, wounded healers must let go of the baggage of guilt, shame, and regret **(Hebrews 12:1)** and embrace the freedom found in Christ.

Wounded Healers pave the way to *harmony of relationship and unity of purpose* addressed through the Kingdom Concepts of: **Disciplined Correction; Mutual Accountability; Cross Reconciliation; Holistic Restoration.**

Wounded Healers serve through their flaws and imperfections as broken vessels that reveal the glory of God with empathy and manage and control their weaknesses to fulfill God's divine design for the lives of those they serve. The Apostle Paul describes the status and condition of those who are considered unworthy and unqualified to serve and lead others in **I Corinthians 1:26-29**, which can be compared to wounded healers.

For [simply] consider your own call, brethren; not many [of you were considered to be] wise according to human estimates and standards, not many influential and powerful, not many of high and noble birth.

[No] for God selected (deliberately chose) what in the world is foolish to put the wise to shame, and what the world calls weak to put the strong to shame.

And God also selected (deliberately chose) what in the world is lowborn and insignificant and branded and treated with contempt, even the things that are nothing, that He might depose and bring to nothing the things that are,

So that no mortal man should [have pretense for glorying and] boast in the presence of God.

XXII. Foundation for Harmony of Relationships and Unity of Purpose

Christ as the Foundation

The core of our faith is Jesus Christ. As stated in **I Corinthians 3:11**, *"For no other foundation can anyone lay than that which is [already] laid, which is Jesus Christ (the Messiah, the Anointed One)."* Christ is the foundation Corner Stone, providing strength and stability to this foundation.

Ephesians 2:20-22 further emphasizes, *"You are built upon the foundation of the apostles and prophets with Christ Jesus Himself the chief Cornerstone. In Him the whole structure is joined (bound, welded) together harmoniously, and it continues to rise (grow, increase) into a holy temple in the Lord [a sanctuary dedicated, consecrated, and sacred to the presence of the Lord]. In Him [and in fellowship with one another] you yourselves also are being built up [into this structure] with the rest, to form a fixed abode (dwelling place) of God in (by, through) the Spirit."*

This foundation is rooted in the teachings of the apostles and prophets, fulfilled in Christ. Believers are called to build upon this foundation with integrity and good works, as **I Corinthians 3:12-13** explains: *"But if anyone builds upon the Foundation, whether it be with gold, silver, precious stones, wood, hay, straw, The work of each [one]* *will become [plainly, openly] known (shown for what it is); for the day [of Christ] will disclose and declare it, because it will be revealed with fire, and the fire will test and critically appraise the character and worth of the work each person has done."*

The focus, then, is on how believers build upon this foundation. Believers are called to build upon this foundation through good works, called precious stones.

—Building God's House Stone by Stone with Good Works—

Spiritual Growth Through Trials and Good Works

Spiritual growth is not possible without encountering and enduring trials, tribulations, and temptations in our everyday experiences. Growth isn't achieved merely by listening to preaching on Sunday morning. Spiritual growth is achieved by living out the application of God's Word in a genuine Christian life, walking a journey that witnesses for Christ through our lifestyle and friendship evangelism. This journey is described in **Romans 5:1-5**, where believers are justified by faith, granted peace with God through Jesus Christ, and rejoice in the hope of God's glory. The passage reminds us that **tribulation** produces **patience**, patience leads to **experience**, experience gives **hope**, and hope does not disappoint and makes us ashamed because God's love is poured into our hearts by the Holy Spirit through what we go through.

As believers pursue righteousness, they may stumble or fall. Thankfully, the grace of God provides a cushion, enabling them to bounce back, though they may need assistance in doing so. This need for help is central to how the Lord's House is constructed—wounded healers must overcome their own brokenness so they can help mend others.

First Building Stone: Disciplined Correction

Correction Produces Discipline That Brings Self Under Spiritual Authority

Within the sacred text of Scripture, we see that God does not judge or condemn His people. Just as the Passover in the Exodus marked the passing over of judgment, Christ, as the Lamb of God, took our place on the cross, so that judgment is not upon us. As stated in **II Corinthians 5:21**, *"For our sake He made Christ [virtually] to be sin Who knew no sin, so that in and through Him we might become [endued with, viewed as being in, and examples of] the righteousness of God [what we ought to be, approved and acceptable and in right relationship with Him, by His goodness]."*

Rather than condemnation, God's Covenant people are corrected by the Spirit, as described in **Hebrews 12:5-29** and **I Corinthians 11:31**. The latter verse highlights that correction is often in the hands of the individual: *"For if we searchingly examined ourselves [detecting our shortcomings and recognizing our own* *condition], we should not be judged and penalty decreed [by the divine judgment]."*

Correction begins with confrontation and admonition against error. Sin is a deviation from the revealed will of God. It is important for believers not to shy away from addressing their errors and the errors of others within the family or the church, even though it may be uncomfortable.

The approach to addressing sin should focus on restoration, not offending others, and encouraging those in error to strive for improvement. Some sins can become addictive, and abrupt changes may not be effective unless the individual is open to transformation by God's grace. It is also important to remain supportive and prayerful, walking with them through their trials, especially when issues stem from family heritage that affect the church community.

Why a Soft Approach Matters

Human nature is frail and prone to both good and evil. All people are vulnerable to experiences that can be **traumatic**, such as **abuse**, **abandonment**, **neglect, rejection**, or **assault**. These wounds cannot be ignored or avoided; they must be confronted directly. Healing requires the removal of the protective bandages that hide the festering problem and demands that we clean out wounds of **anger**, **bitterness**, **vindictiveness**, **hate**, and **deep pain**. While this process is painful, it is necessary and begins with correction that often feels like confrontation, or even interrogation.

Correction is particularly difficult because it is associated with past traumas. The analogy of the oyster is fitting: the irritation caused by a grain of sand eventually produces a pearl. In the same way, the pain of correction can result in healing.

Correction Reveals

Correction brings to light suppressed problems and reveals our readiness or reluctance to face them. It stirs up sensitive emotions tied to our past and family heritage. To mend broken relationships, it is essential to probe our history and have honest conversations about our upbringing, rather than blaming others for our current challenges.

In this context, correction is not about arguing or assigning blame. Emotional issues carry a weight of collective guilt from the past, but God's justice is not focused on who is right or wrong. Each person is accountable for themselves. The emphasis is on initiating reconciliation in the present, as noted in **Matthew 5:23-24**.

Scripture instructs us: ***"Pay attention and always be on your guard [looking out for one another]. If your brother sins (misses the mark), solemnly tell him so and reprove him, and if he repents (feels sorry for having sinned), forgive him. And even if he sins against you seven times in a day, and turns to you seven times and says, I repent [I am sorry], you must forgive him (give up resentment and consider the offense as recalled and annulled)"* (Luke 17:3-4)**.

Forgiving those who have not expressed remorse or repentance can seem impossible, but true forgiveness is reciprocal, between God and us. We would not be forgiven by God if we did not repent. Forgiveness is not about holding grudges or seeking retribution; only God can truly forgive perpetrators. Our role is to repent and forgive before God, creating an opportunity for God to work in their hearts and freeing ourselves from the burden.

—*Forever Forgiveness*—

Forever Forgiveness is realized through a personal relationship with the Lord, grounded in faith and repentance. It focuses on the essentials of faith. Personal repentance and forgiveness do not require contacting everyone who has wronged us, as God can reach those individuals **(Psalms 51:3-4; Matthew 6:14-15)**.

When God forgives us and we forgive others from the heart, He also creates a way to forgive those who have wronged us—even if they are not present. Take the example of Esau forgiving his brother Jacob for stealing his birthright in Genesis chapter 33. Mutual forgiveness between God and the individual is key: if you forgive others, God will also forgive them for their offenses against you.

Unforgiveness is a heavy burden, like carrying a dead weight. Forgiveness liberates us from the penalty and power of past sins, releasing that weight.

Some people who pass through our lives are not significant to God's purpose; they fade from memory because they do not influence God's plan for us. Others, however, are used by God—sometimes through painful experiences—to move us toward our purpose, like Judas, who betrayed Christ. God could have used another means to send Christ to the cross, but Judas played a key role. Rather than dwelling on the reasons for their actions, we should recognize that closure is unnecessary for those who do not affect God's plan. Judas was remorseful almost immediately after he betrayed Christ. Let it go and say goodbye.

Those who require our forgiveness are often close to us and, as part of God's plan, may return to our lives at some point. I've often experienced that. **John 20:23** teaches, *"[Now having received the Holy Spirit, and being led and directed by Him] if you forgive the sins of anyone, they are forgiven; if you retain the sins of anyone, they are retained."* If we do not forgive those near us, we will not experience the fullness of God's forgiveness, and we will continue to carry that burden **(Matthew 6:14-15)**. Remember the words of the Lord in His model perfect prayer: *Forgive us our trespasses as we forgive those who trespass against us.*

Correction as an Opportunity for Dialogue and Healing

Correction is an essential step in God's process of bringing people together to resolve past issues and open doors for further dialogue. The details of these conversations should be based on concrete, agreeable information. Lay the cards (rules) on the table in advance—no surprises. The aim is not to seek apologies or admissions of guilt, but to acknowledge that something went wrong and requires analysis. Effective counseling, like the wisdom of Solomon, involves understanding the person outside of their situation, examining both the circumstances and the contributing factors.

Through correction, the root causes of problems are exposed. Old issues may resurface as participants honestly share their perceptions of past events, recognizing that memory can be unreliable, and stories may change through gossip and rumors. This process can be emotionally painful, but it is necessary for forgiveness and healing. Facing fears through correction paves the way for spiritual and emotional restoration.

When corrections are confronted, both sides are usually skeptical and distrustful. The distrust can reveal itself in several ways: **defensiveness**, **denial**, **anger**, **resentment**, **cynicism**, **sarcasm**, and **apathy**. Some or all of those feelings are normal, but they mask the real problem. They must not stop the process. Dismissal of our animosities will not make them go away. They will only get worse through a historical cycle that repeats the past.

—The Bridge Between the First Building Stone & the Second Building Stone—

To begin connecting the ideas from the *First Building Stone*, it is important to explore the relationship between **Correction** and **Accountability**. Correction serves as a form of discipline, a concept clearly outlined in **Hebrews 12:5-6**: *"And have you [completely] forgotten the divine word of appeal* *and encouragement in which you are reasoned with and addressed as sons? My son, do not think lightly or scorn to submit to the correction and discipline of the Lord, nor lose courage and give up and faint when you are reproved or corrected by Him; For the Lord corrects and disciplines everyone whom He loves, and He punishes, even scourges, every son whom He accepts and welcomes to His heart and cherishes.*

This passage refers back to **Proverbs 3:11-12** and **Proverbs 23:13-14**, which compare chastening to the rod of correction.

Understanding the Rod: Literal or Figurative?

At this point, it is necessary to distinguish between corporal punishment and spiritual discipline. The question arises: Is Solomon, the writer of Proverbs, instructing parents to punish their children, or is he advocating for discipline? Additionally, is the rod mentioned in these scriptures meant to be taken literally, or is it a metaphor?

In some instances, under the Mosaic Law, corporal punishment was indeed used as a harsh response to children who acted in defiance or engaged in unacceptable behaviors. However, the rod (in Hebrew, **"Shebet"** more likely serves as figurative language, representing the shepherd's rod used to guide unruly sheep. This metaphor extends to wayward followers of Christ.

The Shepherd's Rod: Discipline, Not Cruelty

Shepherds traditionally used their staff to gently guide wayward sheep back to the flock, while the rod was reserved for more direct correction. Both Hebrews and Proverbs reference this rod.

The rod was the shepherd's tool for **discipline**, **protection**, and **guidance**—not for inflicting cruel beatings. It would make little sense for a shepherd to beat their sheep or a parent to beat their children, as this would only lead to abuse. Such treatment would render the sheep (or child) docile, vulnerable, passive, and unable to resist threats from predators, or even vindictive toward the enforcer of punishment.

For sheep, these predators might be wolves and serpents. The rod's primary use was to defend against these dangers and to gently nudge the sheep back into safety, preventing them from wandering into harm's way.

This analogy highlights the purpose of divine discipline, which is the central message of these passages in Proverbs and Hebrews.

Divine discipline offers comfort and security to the sheep, ensuring they know the shepherd is present to guide and protect them. Jesus Christ, the **"Good Shepherd,"** leads believers toward **"an abundant life"** through discipline. As stated in **John 10:10**, the main objective of discipline is to protect the flock from danger, not to punish individual sheep out of cruelty.

Divine Discipline and Its Purpose

For followers of Christ, the purpose of discipline is to teach, instruct, and nurture believers for their ultimate good and for God's glory. Those who are disciplined by the Good Shepherd are being led in the way of righteousness.

Divine discipline is distinct from punishment; while parents may punish their children out of anger when they can no longer tolerate misbehavior, God's discipline is not motivated by wrath. Instead, it is an act of love and mercy. God disciplines not because His children have sinned, but because their sins are already forgiven.

When believers endure correction through the challenges of temptation and trials, this endurance serves as evidence that they are truly God's children and not outsiders. Accepting correction and discipline opens believers to accountability—the willingness to acknowledge and confess their errors. This openness is essential in the process of spiritual growth and maturity.

Summary of Correction

The role of correction in spiritual discipline emphasizes its purpose in guiding believers toward righteousness and healing within the context of faith.

- **Correction avoids Condemnation:** God's people are not condemned but corrected by the Spirit to bring self under spiritual authority, with correction often beginning through self-judgment.

- **Correction begins with Confrontation:** Addressing sin involves confronting errors with the goal of restoration, supporting those struggling with sin through prayer and grace.
- **Healing requires gentle Correction:** Human frailty and past trauma necessitate that correction must be approached softly to remove emotional wounds and foster healing, despite the pain involved.
- **Correction reveals hidden Issues:** It exposes suppressed problems tied to past and family heritage, encouraging honest dialogue for reconciliation without blame.
- **Forgiveness is Essential:** Forgiving others, even without their repentance, liberates individuals from burdens and aligns with God's forgiveness, enabling spiritual freedom.
- **Unforgiveness is Burdensome:** Holding onto grudges is compared to carrying dead weight, whereas forgiveness releases the penalty and power of past offenses.
- **Correction facilitates dialogue and Healing:** It opens opportunities for honest conversations to analyze past wrongs and promote spiritual and emotional restoration.
- **Correction often meets Resistance:** Skepticism and distrust are common reactions to correction but must be overcome to prevent repeated harmful cycles.

Divine discipline guides, not punishes: The metaphor of the shepherd's rod illustrates that correction is loving guidance to protect and nurture believers, distinct from punishment, and essential for spiritual growth.

Second Building Stone: Mutual Accountability

Accountability Sacrifices Ego & Selfishness & Releases Humility

The concept of mutual accountability is central to the Christian faith, particularly within both the family and the spiritual community, often referred to as the Body of Christ. Scripture passages such as **I Corinthians 11:3**, **Ephesians 5:22-33**; **6:1-9**, and **I Corinthians 12:4-28** collectively emphasize that accountability is not limited to one direction or hierarchy. Instead, it is shared among all members, regardless of their roles or status.

Accountability is about Honor and Respect for People and not mere Positions.

True accountability is a transformative quality that involves setting aside one's ego and selfish desires. Embracing accountability means opening oneself to humility, recognizing that individual interests must sometimes yield for the sake of unity and respect within the family community and the community of faith. Therefore, accountability is not measured in the Christian community by elevated authority. The highest authority is Christ. Leaders and followers are the same in the eyes of God's judicial righteousness, except for varying gifts. (The ministry positions in Ephesians 4:11-

12 are described as "gifts" to equip the Body of Believers.) Whether in a family or the Family of God, when we have personal preferences based on those we perceive as better, we are actually out of authority and unaccountable.

There is a tendency in human nature to disregard those of low status and become offensive to them, but we must see everyone in the Body of Christ as the same. That scenario is fleshed out in **I Corinthians 12:4-28**, where Paul uses the analogy of human anatomy and physiology to illustrate the significance of the foot, the hand, the eye, and the ear to the functioning of the whole body. Then he points out in **verses 23-25** that the parts of our body that we think are less significant should be given more attention than those parts of the body that need no attention, so all parts are significant. His point in **verse 25** is that there should be no division in the Body.

—*Servant Leaders: Motivation and Example*—

The servant leader's primary motivation is to serve from the bottom up. Christ didn't come from glory to an ivory tower; He came from a humble, blue-collar, working-class family.

Mary and Joseph traveled to Bethlehem to register for the census in crowded conditions. Mary was in her ninth month of pregnancy, and the text says *there was no room in the inn*. The traditional interpretation of this passage, without considering the historical context, suggests that the inn had no vacancy.

Although Joseph and Mary lived in Nazareth, Joseph's ancestral home was Bethlehem, which could mean he may have had extended families in Bethlehem during the time of the taxation census.

Inns were not like our contemporary inns today. The Greek word *"kataluma"* is better translated as *"guest room"* or *"lodging place,"* which indicates Joseph and Mary may have been turned away from an extended family member's home, not simply because of crowded conditions, and were given lodging away from their household in the cellar, where the animals were lodged. If that were true, it could mean that relatives could have made room for a distant relative through Joseph, out of concern for her well-being, seeing that she was about to deliver her baby. But that remains speculation and conjecture. Regardless of the circumstances, it was prophesied that Christ would be born in Bethlehem **(Micah 5:2-5)**, but the baby Jesus being placed in a feeding trough for animals after His birth is not mentioned. However, when we compare the languages of other Scriptures, like Nathanael's words in **John 1:46**, *"Nathanael answered him, [Nazareth!] Can anything good come out of Nazareth? Philip replied, Come and see!"* suggesting that Nazareth was a type of backward community of unlearned, immoral people, and the prophecies of **Isaiah 53,** where Christ is described as ***despised and rejected of men***, it could mean they were unwelcome. But again, that has no bearing on the text. But it does give us something to think about when it comes to disregard for less fortunate people, poor people, and stereotypes about them as bad people. Salvation focuses on all people, with emphasis on those considered the worst of the worst, and accountability is not just about people considered less than us; we are also accountable to them.

Think of this for a moment: If Christ came first to a rich family, do you think His ministry would have trickled down to the poor? Let that sink in and reflect on His words at the inception of His public ministry. *"The Spirit of the Lord [is] upon Me, because He has anointed Me [the Anointed One, the Messiah] to preach the good news (the Gospel) to the poor; He has sent Me to announce release to the captives and recovery of sight to the blind, to send forth as delivered those who are oppressed [who are downtrodden, bruised, crushed, and broken down by calamity],"* (Luke 4:18).

Contrast with Traditional Secular Leadership

Traditional leadership, especially within worldly systems, is characterized by power and hierarchical control. In contrast, servant leadership operates on the spiritual principle of prioritizing the well-being and success of those served above the leader's own interests. **Philippians 2:3-5** instructs, *"Do nothing from factional motives [through contentiousness, strife, selfishness, or for unworthy ends] or prompted by conceit and empty arrogance. Instead, in the true spirit of humility (lowliness of mind) let each regard the others as better than and superior to* *himself [thinking more highly of one another than you do of yourselves].*

Let each of you esteem and look upon and be concerned for not [merely] his own interests, but also each for the interests of others.

Let this same attitude and purpose and [humble] mind be in you which was in Christ Jesus: [Let Him be your example in humility:]"

This principle emphasizes humility and unselfishness, requiring a commitment to serving others in a Christ-like manner.

Peter, in **I Peter 5:5**, further encourages the Christian community to submit to one another and to be clothed with humility: *"Likewise, you who are younger and of lesser rank, be subject to the elders (the ministers and spiritual guides of the church)—[giving them due respect and yielding to their counsel]. Clothe (apron) yourselves, all of you, with humility [as the garb of a servant, so that its covering cannot possibly be stripped from you, with freedom from pride and arrogance] toward one another. For God sets Himself against the proud (the insolent, the overbearing, the disdainful, the presumptuous, the boastful)—[and He opposes, frustrates, and defeats them], but gives grace (favor, blessing) to the humble."*

Servant leadership is marked by humility given by grace, which enables accountability to the Lord. The servant leader delegates authority to the Lord for subjection, serving by example, and being subject first to the Lord, as illustrated in **I Corinthians 11:1**: *"Pattern yourselves after me [follow my example], as I imitate and follow Christ (the Messiah)."* Restoring unity in families and churches requires those who desire reconciliation to demonstrate humility, openness, and a willingness to be corrected.

Grace and Humility Empower Others

A servant leader's measure of success is found not in personal achievements but in the empowerment of others.

Through discipleship, transparency about personal flaws, and investment in the growth of others, servant leaders encourage individuals to take on new responsibilities and roles.

Throughout my pastorate, I prioritized granting leaders' freedom to serve within the corporate vision. However, it is important to approach leadership selection through a careful vetting process. Even with such diligence, there is no guarantee that those empowered will not misuse their authority. For instance, in my urban church start-up, some appointed leaders began to assert their own visions and spread negative comments about my leadership within their groups. The New Testament addresses such rebellion, referencing it in **Jude 1:11** as **"the rebellion of Korah"** and in **II Timothy 3:8** regarding opponents of Moses, Jannes and Jambres.

Accountability is Essential for Unity and Reconciliation

Servant leaders view their role as removing obstacles and supporting those they serve, enabling their growth and performance. Their focus is on personal and professional development, empowerment, active listening, building trust, and strong relationships. They act as stewards of resources for those they serve, taking a long-term perspective on their service by maintaining a holistic awareness of ethics, power dynamics, and values. Empathy and a commitment to healing further distinguish servant leadership from traditional models.

—Contrasting Accountability: Worldly Systems vs. Kingdom Principles—

Accountability in worldly systems can involve imposed control, sometimes against a person's will. In the kingdom of God, accountability is characterized by voluntary submission to Christ through the network of believers. Loyalty to the Lord forms the basis for this accountability, while submission to human authority should be guided by integrity and honesty. Jeremiah's words in **Jeremiah 17:5** warn against placing ultimate trust in human leaders: *"Thus says the Lord: Cursed [with great evil] is the strong man who trusts in and relies on frail man, making weak [human] flesh his arm, and whose mind and heart turn aside from the Lord."*

God's grace enables believers to **respect** and **honor** those in the community of faith and those over us in employment in worldly systems without compromising integrity.

Ultimately, accountability to the Lord should be the standard by which actions and words are measured, whether within the church or in broader society.

Accountability is Based on Relationships

Accountability is rooted in relationships and is defined as the state of being answerable for one's conduct, especially when it has negatively affected others. Whether as public officials, religious leaders, family members, or friends, individuals are accountable to a higher authority when the Moral Law is violated. The Ten Commandments, known as the Ten Words, provide a framework for relationships with God and others—four commandments focus on our relationship with the Lord, while six address relationships with people.

For believers, God in Christ is the ultimate authority. Outside of a legal context, accountability to others cannot be coerced but must be freely accepted. This is why confronting issues through correction is the initial step, allowing individuals the opportunity to come forward and address breaches in relationships.

For accountability to work properly, relationships must be aligned in an orderly manner with respect and honor.

During my pastorate, I relegated my authority to supervision because I believe that relegating our authority is like removing ourselves from a circle. Imagine a circle with a stick person in the center and other stick people around the edges of the circle. Strings are tying the hands, feet, and heads of the stick people around the edge of the circle to the person in the center of the circle. It means that they can't think or move without the person in the center thinking and moving first because they control the circle. That becomes micro-managing management, which will offend and eventually fall apart. Now, imagine the person in the center detaching themselves from the people in the circle and stepping outside of the circle. That's relegation that frees those on the edge of the circle to use their unique talents and abilities to perform the tasks given to them by the supervisor outside of the circle. Accountability occurs when those in the circle and outside of the circle mutually respect and honor each other's roles. That action connects them to **correction** and the third stone, **reconciliation**.

Accountability Affirms Reconciliation and Responsibility

Every person is ultimately accountable to the Lord on the Day of Reckoning and within their own conscience when convicted of a breach in relationship. The human conscience acts as its own judge and jury on behalf of God, urging individuals to seek reconciliation. In the present, each person must answer to their own conscience when under conviction, and no one else can make that decision for them.

Accountability sets the stage for constructive action, guiding participants in the right direction. It is both a legal and moral responsibility for the welfare and care of others, especially family members, even when there is no obligation. Taking responsibility fosters mutual obligations and increases the likelihood of meaningful action to address issues.

The process of accountability explores problems that hinder personal growth. Its goal is edification and spiritual equality—common ground as described in **Philippians 2:1-5**.

Accountability lifts participants out of neutrality, prompting them to become stewards to resolve issues. This process requires personal sacrifice, which is the equivalent of "bearing our cross," or dying to our selfishness, which may be challenging but is essential for building bridges of reconciliation. Sacrifice can involve time, adjusting schedules, postponing leisure, traveling for forums, or listening intently to someone's story.

As **Romans 14:11-12** states, *"For it is written, As I live, says the Lord, every knee shall bow to Me, and every tongue shall confess to God [acknowledge Him to His honor and to His praise]. And so each of us shall give an account of himself [give an answer in reference to judgment] to God."*

Mutual Accountability Summary

Mutual accountability in the Christian context involves shared responsibility and humility among all members of families and faith communities, emphasizing honor and respect for people with regard to positions of authority. This concept fosters unity, reconciliation, and servant leadership modeled after Christ's example.

- **Mutual accountability in Christian Life:** Accountability is shared among all members of the family and spiritual community, not limited by hierarchy or status. It requires humility and setting aside selfish desires for unity and respect.

- **Equality within the Body of Christ:** Every member, regardless of perceived status, is essential and should be treated with equal care to avoid division and prejudice, as illustrated by the analogy of the human body in 1 Corinthians 12.

- **Servant leadership Motivation:** Servant leaders prioritize serving others from the bottom up, exemplified by Christ's humble birth and life, emphasizing service over power or comfort.

- **Contrast with secular Leadership:** Unlike traditional hierarchical leadership, servant leadership focuses on humility, unselfishness, and valuing others above oneself, as taught in Philippians and 1 Peter.

- **Empowerment through Grace and Humility:** Success for servant leaders is measured by empowering others through discipleship and transparency, though challenges such as misuse of authority may arise.

- **Accountability fosters Unity and Reconciliation:** Servant leaders support growth, build trust, and practice empathy, distinguishing their approach from worldly leadership models characterized by control.

- **Kingdom versus Worldly Accountability:** Christian accountability is voluntary submission to Christ and loyalty to God, contrasting with imposed control in secular systems, with ultimate accountability to the Lord.

- **Accountability rooted in Relationships:** Accountability involves being answerable for one's conduct, guided by respect and honor within relationships, and leads to correction, responsibility, and reconciliation, ultimately before God.

Third Building Stone: Cross Reconciliation

Friendships Create Opportunity for Restoration

Cross Reconciliation is an important mandate derived from the Gospel and the Great Commission, as described in **Matthew 28:18-20**. However, it is not the sole mandate. The central mandate is to reconcile broken and fallen humanity to God through Jesus Christ. This is clearly stated in **II Corinthians 5:20**: *"So we are Christ's ambassadors, God making His appeal as it were through us. We [as Christ's personal representatives] beg you for His sake to lay hold of the divine favor [now offered you] and be reconciled to God."*

The ministry of reconciliation extends beyond reconciling humanity to God; it also encompasses cross-cultural reconciliation among different ethnicities separated by cultural differences. **Ephesians 2:12-16** highlights the hostility and mutual enmity that existed between Jews and Gentiles, showing how Christ has removed this enmity through His sacrifice on the cross.

The cross of Christ is powerful in breaking down the dividing walls that separate races, ethnicities, and cultures. However, this unity does not occur automatically. Disciples of Christ must take responsibility and actively engage in reconciling people to one another through Christ. As stated in **II Corinthians 5:18**, *"But all things are from God, Who through Jesus Christ reconciled us to Himself [received us into favor, brought us into harmony with Himself] and gave to us the ministry of reconciliation [that by word and deed we might aim to bring others into harmony with Him]."*

Reconciliation: The Heart of the Covenant Promise

Reconciliation lies at the core of God's covenant promise. **Jeremiah 31:33** says, *"But this is the covenant which I will make with the house of Israel: After those days, says the Lord, I will put My law within them, and on their hearts will I write it; and I will be their God, and they will be My people."*

While the specific term "reconciliation" does not appear in Old Testament manuscripts, its concept is drawn from the Greco-Roman world. The Apostle Paul likely adopted the term from the nature of covenant agreements rooted in God's promise to Israel.

The Hebrew word for covenant, **"běriyth,"** implies a cutting or passing between the flesh of an animal, where the blood of the covenant provides atonement for trespasses. This mutual agreement can be understood as a model for reconciliation between individuals or parties, where atonement covers breaches in relationships.

In Greek, **"katallage"** is the word for reconciliation. When individuals are reconciled to God through the Good News, they receive the gift of reconciliation and are empowered to restore relationships with others within the Body of Christ as well as those outside it. Every disciple, therefore, has a ministry of reconciliation and a responsibility to resolve breaches in relationships as peacemakers. Reconciliation requires conviction of conscience—if accountability is lacking, reconciliation is difficult to achieve.

Reconciliation as a Path to Unity

Scripture teaches that reconciliation creates the opportunity for harmony and unity of purpose in relationships. This is illustrated in **Matthew 18:18-20**, where Jesus says:

Truly I tell you, whatever you forbid and declare to be improper and unlawful on earth must be what is already forbidden in heaven, and whatever you permit and declare proper and lawful on earth must be what is already permitted in heaven.

Again I tell you, if two of you on earth agree (harmonize together, make a symphony together) about whatever [anything and everything] they may ask, it will come to pass and be done for them by My Father in heaven.

For wherever two or three are gathered (drawn together as My followers) in (into) My name, there I Am in the midst of them.

The keyword **"agree"** in **verse 19** comes from a musical term for harmony, suggesting that the Lord is the Maestro orchestrating unified relationships. Unity of purpose is essential.

In the historical context, Old Testament aldermen (city councilmen) who met at the city gate required unanimous agreement for legislation to pass. (Meeting at the city gates represented the key to controlling what went into the city.) There was no such thing as agreeing to disagree. Disagreement meant the issue would be tabled until consensus was reached. Relatively, if two or three believers agree on God's Kingdom Mandate, God sanctions that agreement in Heaven and brings it to fruition on Earth. (Numbers in our world systems are not measured by numbers in the Kingdom of God. God uses fewer numbers in the Kingdom to override more numbers in our worldly systems.) First, reconciliation must be achieved between those praying for the cause of Christ. The question remains: Do we truly believe this principle?

Ethnicity, Culture, and the Development of Diversity

Ethnicity is understood as family heritage, not racial classification. Culture emerges as ethnic families migrate and adapt to their environments, developing distinct norms and values. This diversity is not a matter of superiority but reflects different ways of living—language, dress, thought, articulation, worship, fellowship, service, and outreach. The early development of ethnicities and cultures is recorded in **Genesis 11**.

After the flood (postdiluvian period), people shared a common culture **(Genesis 11:1)**. The emergence of diverse cultures followed the changing of languages at the Tower of Babel. Initially, differences were not defined by race but by clan and genealogy, allowing for multiethnic coexistence. **Genesis 10:32** states: *"These are the families of the sons of Noah, according to their generations, within their nations; and from these the nations spread abroad on the earth after the flood."*

The Descendants of Shem

The migrations of Shem's lineage are detailed in **Genesis 10:21-31**. Various descendants migrated to regions such as northern Turkey, Syria, Iran, Iraq, Saudi Arabia, and Ethiopia. The direct line from Shelah and Eber led to the ancient Hebrews, originating in central/north Saudi Arabia. The descendants of Shem settled in Mediterranean climates, becoming shepherds and nomadic farmers.

The Descendants of Ham

Ham's descendants, the largest people group of the three, as described in **Genesis 10:6-20**, migrated to southern Egypt, Libya, Palestine, Ethiopia, Egypt, Saudi Arabia, and Yemen. The descendants of Ham lived in hot, arid climates, jungles, and rainforests, and under Nimrod's leadership, became urban dwellers and city builders.

The Descendants of Japheth

Japheth's descendants settled along the coastlands of Indo-Europe. Migrations stretched to areas now known as Ukraine, Iran, Greece, Turkey, Italy, and along the Mediterranean and Black Sea coasts. They settled in cooler, oceanic climates and became seafaring nations.

The climate and migration patterns influenced the complexion of these peoples. Names and descriptions in scripture suggest distinctions such as "dusky" (Shem), "fair" (Japheth), and possibly "black" (Ham). Nevertheless, God's call is not to judge superficial differences but to reconcile them, following Christ's example in **John 4**. Jesus crossed cultural, racial, and religious boundaries to reach and reconcile the Samaritan woman, demonstrating the power of reconciliation.

—*Resolving Conflict: The Pathway to Reconciliation*—

Conflict arises when two people try to occupy the same space. To resolve conflict, it is necessary to expand the space and accommodate the other person, redrawing or erasing dividing lines. The phrase "bury the hatchet," originating from Native American traditions, symbolizes the act of making peace by literally burying weapons. This process involves several steps:

1. Be open-minded about the offense.
2. Accept apologies with conviction that expresses, "I'm sorry" if you believe it, or move directly to forgiveness if not.
3. Forgive the other person.
4. Pursue peace actively.

God never intended conflict to divide His people or families. Instead, conflict highlights problems and offers opportunities for reconciliation.

Lifestyle Friendship Evangelism

Friendship, exemplified by Christ in **John 15:15**, involves gradually sharing one's life and experiences with like-minded individuals. Jesus said, *"I do not call you servants (slaves) any longer, for the servant does not know what his master is doing (working out). But I have called you My friends, because I have made known to you everything that I have heard from My Father. [I have revealed to you everything that I have learned from Him.]"* Friendship is the open sharing of emotions. However, it is wise to exercise caution in sharing personal matters, as premature disclosure can lead to misunderstanding or harm.

Deep personal issues should be disclosed only when the situation is appropriate, and for severe trauma or abuse, professional therapy is recommended rather than group sharing.

Building friendship is a gradual process, like peeling an onion—deeper layers may reveal more painful issues. What is shared should align with God's view, not merely others' opinions.

Commitment to a Reconciled Covenant Relationship

Reconciliation involves committing to a covenant relationship and crossing boundaries that divide, thereby building bridges between differences. True friendship for believers is rooted in a covenant relationship with the Lord and one another, serving as a means to heal breaches in relationships.

Reconciliation: Getting to Know Each Other

Understanding Reconciliation Through Relationship

Before we can truly understand one another, it is essential that we first take the time to genuinely get to know each other. Attempting to understand someone without this foundation often leads to misunderstandings. Building relationships over time creates trust and knowledge necessary for a deeper understanding by sharing our histories. When we first came to the Lord, our knowledge of Him was limited. However, as we continued to grow spiritually through the study of God's Word, our understanding of the Lord became richer and more detailed.

The Simplicity of Reconciliation

Reconciliation does not need to be a complicated process. At its core, it is about getting to know each other through **acceptance**, **embracing**, and **celebration** of our differences. Here, the focus is on neutral differences—those aspects of culture such as food, clothing, language, and behavior patterns that are not inherently right or wrong, but simply unique to each group. It is important to recognize that reconciliation does not mean amalgamation or integration, where one culture is absorbed into another. Instead, it is about respecting and valuing these differences.

Biblical Example: Acts 15 and the Reconciliation Conference

A key biblical example of reconciliation is found in **Acts 15**, during the first Reconciliation Conference that sought to unite Jews and Gentiles. Judaizers—Jewish Christians—insisted that newly converted Gentiles and church communities from Indo-European backgrounds must conform to Mosaic customs to be considered true Christians. Paul and the chief Apostles rejected this demand, instead advising only that Gentile believers abstain from idolatry and extramarital sex. All other cultural norms were accepted, demonstrating the principle of embracing neutral differences.

Cultural Diversity in God's Kingdom

Even in God's glorious Kingdom, our cultural differences will remain. Scripture supports this idea, referencing every tribe, language, nation, and people in **Revelation 5:9**, **Revelation 7:9**, and **Revelation 14:6-7**. **Revelation 21:24** further describes how the kings of the earth will bring their glory and honor into the New Jerusalem, symbolically offering their earthly achievements and powers to God in praise. As **Psalm 24:1** states, ***"The earth is the LORD'S, and the fulness thereof; the world, and they that dwell therein."*** This affirms that diversity is not only accepted but celebrated in the presence of God.

Fourth Building Stone: Holistic Restoration

Holistic Restoration Produces Peace & Wholeness

Holistic Restoration centers on the comprehensive health and well-being of an individual, encompassing their physical, mental, and emotional states—all of which originate from spiritual well-being.

This journey begins with the human spirit, described as the God-consciousness within. When a person chooses to follow Christ, the process of holistic restoration is initiated, starting with the transformation of their inner spirit. Personally, after coming to Christ, my life progressively improved under the guidance of God's Spirit living within me, leading to my present circumstances. I now experience greater happiness (the joy of the Lord), enjoy robust health for someone of seventy-five years, maintain physical fitness, possess sharper mental faculties with strong memory recall, and benefit from emotional stability and financial contentment. I am at peace with myself and with God, and this state of well-being has empowered me to form meaningful relationships with people from diverse backgrounds without prejudice or judgment.

Reciprocity versus Restitution

It is important to acknowledge that science can be aligned with God's Word, though not the other way around; God's Word need not conform to science.

Higher Truth originates from above. Within this framework, reciprocity—a form of retribution resulting in losses, and restitution, the restoration of what was lost is both rooted in the fixed divine laws of the universe, operating under God's Providence. God watches over and supervises the universe and our world.

Some may separate their faith from science, choosing not to believe in the latter. That is acceptable, as clarity will come in time, as foretold in the Book of Revelation. On the human level, reciprocity means that our actions, whether good or bad, return to us, following the principle of **"sowing and reaping" (Galatians 6:7-10)**. Restitution, the opposite of reciprocity, allows for gains—exponential blessings as described in **Psalms 1**. The focus is less on losses and more on the gains available in the Lord. Still, both losses and gains are influenced by our choices.

Reciprocity and restitution, as fixed laws set by the Creator, operate automatically on two levels: **nature** and **human nature**. When these laws are disrupted—such as when the ecological balance is disturbed for profit or endangered species are destroyed for personal gain—nature's food chain is interrupted, leading to chaos in the system. This results in collateral damage to natural resources and triggers "climate change" as a result of exploiting natural resources. The latter can manifest as storms and extreme events across earth, water, air, and fire, potentially escalating into geo-storms. Scripture teaches that God, in His infinite power, manages and oversees all occurrences in the universe, delegating authority to humanity for the consequences of their actions **(Colossians 1:16-17; Hebrews 1:1-2)**.

Through Divine Providence, God sustains all things. In alignment with these fixed laws, the outcomes of justice and judgment can be observed in the laws of physics—specifically, **"cause and effect,"** which parallels the biblical principles of "sowing and reaping" **(Galatians 6:7-10)** and "restitution."

The Process of Restitution

Restoration involves retributive compensation for losses suffered due to inequitable or unjust actions. Disparities caused by human greed often result in individuals being deprived of just compensation for their labor. This concept is evident in prophetic scripture and many of Christ's parables: the unjust judge (Luke 18), the workers in the vineyard (Matthew 20:1-16), the parable of the talents—especially the servant who buried his talent (Matthew 25:14-30), the unforgiving servant (Matthew 18:21-35), and the shrewd manager (Luke 16:1-13). Additional passages, such as I Timothy 6:10, 13-14, warn of the corrupting influence of the love of money and urge the wealthy to share with those in need. The most serious admonition against the rich exploiting the poor is found in **James 5:1-8**, where God declares that He will judge the rich and compensate the poor.

A Better Quality of Life

While injustice often leads to loss, and those responsible will face the consequences of their actions, the opportunity for gain lies with those who have suffered. It is important not to harbor resentment or expect the world to compensate us without our own efforts to improve our circumstances.

Christ's promise, found in the Covenant provision, assures **"an abundant life."** In **John 10**, Jesus says, *"The thief comes only in order to steal and kill and destroy. I came that they may have and enjoy life, and have it in abundance (to the full, till it overflows)."* This means a better quality of life, allowing for greater contributions to the Kingdom of God as faithful stewards, ultimately resulting in exponential blessings. The more we give to the cause of Christ—whether time, resources, or service—the more God will bless us, enabling us to continue giving. This is the essence of restoration: being made whole physically, mentally, emotionally, relationally, and financially.

Strengthening Relationships Through Restoration and Fellowship

Restoration Fortifies the Bridge of Relationships

Restoration is essential to giving permanence and strength to our relationships. It means that true friends do not need to be constantly present in each other's lives for the relationship to endure. Reflecting on my own experiences, especially with cross-cultural partners, I have learned that an authentic connection cannot be forced. At times, others insisted on being actively involved in my life, which began to feel like an imposition rather than a genuine friendship. My lifelong philosophy has remained consistent: love and friendship cannot be compelled. I often illustrate this with the image of a caged bird; when you open the cage and set the bird free, if it returns, it is yours—if not, it was never yours to begin with. This analogy highlights that a meaningful friendship is about being there in times of need, rather than being present constantly or forced into closeness. **Friendship needs to be encouraged by words and deeds to head in the right direction.** Therefore, we should not have unrealistic expectations about friendship, as doing so may lead to disappointment.

Fellowship Builds Relationships

For believers, the bonds formed in this life are given an enduring quality by the promise of eternal life. Whether or not we see our friends again in this world, we are assured of knowing one another in the life to come. This assurance comes through the unity of fellowship, which brings lasting value to relationships.

The Greek word for fellowship, "koinonia," conveys a meaning much deeper than that of a mere social connection. Unlike secular relationships, which are often superficial and fragile, koinonia is defined by communion with the Lord and shared life within the Body of Christ. The foundation of this fellowship is Christlikeness, which creates an unbreakable spiritual bond. Through this bond, God uses His people to mutually support and rebuild one another, especially in times of need.

Throughout my ministry journey, I have benefited greatly from the generosity and support of others, especially my cross-cultural partners. Their help has been instrumental in rebuilding my life after seasons of loss and missed opportunities. Circumstances and people may have held me back, but the encouragement and assistance I received propelled my life forward. The list of blessings is extensive: a gifted car when I was first saved, fundraising efforts for building projects, ministry opportunities, financial gifts to support my household, increased compensation in ministry, and free professional services such as dental and medical care, as well as donated vacations. There are countless examples of how others have contributed to my journey. Importantly, I never regarded these as acts of charity; rather, my faith and works enabled the Lord to bless me and inspire others to support my ministry, all because of the integrity of the vision. To experience restitution, our lives must reflect vision and purpose that the Lord is willing to honor. As **Philippians 4:19** says, *"And my God will liberally supply (fill to the full) your every need according to His riches in glory in Christ Jesus."*

Scriptural Foundations of Restoration and Restitution

The story of **Zacchaeus** in **Luke 19** offers a powerful example of restoration and restitution. Zacchaeus, a wealthy tax collector, was so eager to see Jesus that he climbed a tree because he couldn't see over the crowd due to his short height. Jesus noticed him and invited him to come down. Moved by conviction, Zacchaeus responded, *"So then Zacchaeus stood up and solemnly declared to the Lord, See, Lord, the half of my goods I [now] give [by way of restoration] to the poor, and if I have cheated anyone out of anything, I [now] restore four times as much."* **(Luke 19:8,9a)**. Christ concluded that it was the result of redemption. The story of the **"Good Samaritan"** in **Luke 10:25-37** also reflects the meaning of restitution.

Restitution begins at the very start of the Christian journey and reaches its fulfillment in God's Kingdom, where unimaginable wealth, glorified immortal bodies, eternal rewards—symbolized as crowns—and everlasting joy await. **Acts 3:21** refers to this as the restitution of all things. In the meantime, God promises to restore the years lost by being outside His will, as noted in **Joel 2:25**. Here, Israel, a nation dependent on agriculture, suffered loss due to disobedience, resulting in failed harvests. Similarly, believers today experience the blessings of Abraham in Christ, receiving reciprocity and restitution through God's faithfulness when they obey God's Word, which is His Will.

The Result: Restoration Brings Peace and Permanence

Restoration strengthens the bridge of reconciliation by actively seeking to rebuild relationships and secure their permanence, even among diverse individuals. It creates an atmosphere of peace through God's presence. Restoration is the intentional action we take to rebuild our own lives and to help rebuild the lives of others. When we engage in restoration, we bring lasting peace to our relationships. Friendships endure and remain strong, even when friends are separated by distance or circumstance.

Conclusion
Pathway to Higher Truth—Cleansing of the Soul
Exploring Ultimate Reality & the Journey to Heaven

This work sets forth a pragmatic approach to understanding and experiencing higher truth. The central emphasis is on making the profound teachings of the sacred text of Scripture accessible and relevant to everyday life. The principle of **"God-talk"** guides this process, fostering spiritual conversations that are firmly rooted in real-life experiences. Here, individuals are encouraged to explore spiritual matters freely, drawing their own conclusions rather than being compelled to accept established doctrines or theological frameworks.

In this context, theology is stripped down to its essence: humanity's concept of God is thoughtfully weighed against the Word of God, much like the many facets of a diamond contribute to its brilliance. Achieving higher truth is therefore seen as a journey—one that involves considering multiple perspectives across five distinct **faith steps**. This approach empowers individuals to thoughtfully evaluate these perspectives and arrive at their personal understanding.

God's Truth as Ultimate Reality

According to Scripture, the Kingdom of God represents the ultimate reality toward which the world is moving.

From the standpoint of Creation Science, time can be understood as eternity being slowed down, allowing human experience to unfold. The Genesis account reveals that God created time out of eternity, a concept that can be considered alongside modern scientific theories such as the Big Bang. When God spoke creation into existence, it is conceivable that a tremendous sound filled heaven, bringing forth a luminous Quasar of light from darkness. The formation of the heavens, as well as the plant and animal kingdoms, may have developed over time rather than within a single 24-hour period.

While linguistic and exegetical studies can provide insights into the meaning of Scripture, certain aspects of God's creative work will remain mysteries—waiting for revelation in eternity. The **Lord's Prayer**, as recorded in **Matthew 6:9-13** and **Luke 11:2-4**, encompasses the deepest human needs, expressing the hope: **"Thy kingdom come, thy will be done on earth as it is in heaven**.*"* This means that God's ultimate reality is destined to manifest on earth as time progresses, and it is only a matter of time before the fullness of God's Kingdom is revealed here.

Believers are described as citizens of God's Kingdom **(Philippians 3:20)**, living as disciples and sojourners, much like Abraham, who journeyed in search of a city with eternal foundations built by God **(Hebrews 11:9-10)**. As members of this kingdom, believers are called to embody its principles, as taught in the Beatitudes **(Matthew 5:3-11)** and throughout the Sermon on the Mount **(Matthew 5-7)**.

The Journey to Eternity

A common thread running through all religions is the belief that time exists between two eternities and that humanity is moving along a path toward eternal fulfillment or bliss. There are, however, divergent views. Some atheists, for example, reject the existence of God and consider the soul to be mortal. In this view, the soul perishes at death and passes into oblivion, with consciousness understood as a function of the physical brain that ceases when the brain no longer functions. Science, based on empirical evidence and experimentation, does not confirm the imperishability of the soul or its survival after death; thus, there is no scientific evidence for its continued existence.

Major Religious Perspectives on the Afterlife

There are three major world religions—**Christianity**, **Judaism**, and **Islam**—all of which trace their heritage to Abraham and believe in the One God, through different names and understand God in distinct ways.

In Christianity, God is revealed through Christ; in Judaism, through YHWH and Adonai; and in Islam, as Allah. Each tradition offers its own path to heaven or eternal life:

- **Christianity:** Eternal life and entry into heaven are made possible by faith in Christ's completed work of salvation, accomplished through His cross.

- **Judaism:** The way to eternal life, or Olam Ha-Ba (the world to come), is pursued through righteous living according to the mitzvot (commandments), teshuva (repentance), and tzedakah (charity). After death, there may be a period of purification called Gehinnom.

- **Islam:** The path to Jannah (paradise) involves a combination of faith in God, righteous actions, performing daily prayers, fasting, charity, and observing holy days.

Most religions affirm some form of life after death, but the nature and attainment of that life differ widely among traditions. The central question is how one achieves life after death. Ultimately, each path to heaven—across various religions—requires faith. However, these paths are not presented as equally valid routes; rather, each tradition claims a unique way. If there were multiple ways to heaven, it would suggest the existence of many gods, leading to a pantheon and, ultimately, to idolatry.

Clear Thinking and Holistic Healing
Releasing Your Faith

Clear thinking is essential for authentic faith, as it helps remove mental and emotional filters that can obstruct belief and trust. The Apostle Paul calls it **"Reckoning,"** meaning mental ascent: to raise your consciousness to the truth of Scripture, even when you don't fully understand it, to invigorate your faith. One example is in **Romans 6:11**. *"Even so consider yourselves also dead to sin and your relation to it broken, but alive to God [living in unbroken fellowship with Him] in*

Christ Jesus." Recognize that your old nature (old man) has been judicially crucified with Christ. I have developed five steps toward this kind of clarity, which enable us to overcome the barriers that limit our faith.

My own faith is rooted not in traditional historical Christianity, but in the foundational truths of the untranslated sacred text. In this context, the concept of going to heaven is understood as a gift of eternal life—one that does not depend on performing good works or deeds to obtain it. However, good works do have their significance: they earn believers rewards at the Judgment Seat of Christ, as described in **II Corinthians 5:10**.

The transformation of our lives is the result of Christ's redemptive work on the cross, which, through God's Word and Spirit, guarantees heaven for us despite our failures, faults, and shortcomings. This assurance does not mean we have a license to misuse God's grace or intentionally continue in sin, as emphasized in **Romans 6:1**. The epistles of John teach that it is impossible for the nature of God's Spirit within us to practice ongoing sin, though we may still make mistakes or even go through periods of spiritual struggle. As previously outlined, where there is faith, there is Christ; where there is Christ, there is life; and where there is life, there is a lifestyle that reflects that life.

True believers remain in Christ until they meet the Lord in eternity, inspired and encouraged by the knowledge of Christ, which brings holistic healing and motivates us to live better lives.

Holistic Healing Takes Time

Healing is a process that unfolds over time. Sometimes it happens quickly, but often it is a gradual journey rather than an immediate event, like the miraculous healings recorded in Scripture. Those moments are miracles—divine interventions that interrupt the normal course of life. Similarly, the born-again experience of a believer is itself a miracle, one that cannot be explained by human logic. We are encouraged to believe in miracles, but when healing does not occur according to our expectations, it is not because of any fault in God or a deficiency in our faith.

God's wisdom is seen in the thoroughness of healing that takes place over time. As we are healed psychologically, emotionally, and spiritually from what may be psychosomatic (false) illnesses caused by anxiety, trauma, and suppressed pain, we experience wholeness in spirit, soul, and body. This sense of being made whole starts and ends with forgiveness: receiving forgiveness from God, extending forgiveness to ourselves and to those who have hurt us, and seeking forgiveness from those we have wronged.

True healing is evident when we can speak openly about past pain—whether related to people or circumstances—without feeling anger or resentment deep within us. If there is still pain and anger, it means the healing process must continue, possibly by following the steps outlined here.

Healing is a Cleansing Process

Healing can be compared to taking a shower in refreshing water, washing away the dirt of life's problems. Leprosy, as an example, is a debilitating and progressively worsening disease if left untreated. Trauma and the toxic pain of the past operate similarly: if not addressed, they worsen over time. Leprosy is highly contagious, and so are untreated traumas and past pain, though in a different way. Our own "leprosy"—the pain and trauma within—can affect those around us through the negative attitudes we project, creating an atmosphere that drives people away. In modern terms, this can manifest as "ghosting" or "gaslighting," leading to social isolation much like the lepers of the past.

Just as those afflicted with leprosy were separated from society in leper colonies, people burdened by unresolved trauma often isolate themselves from family, friends, and the wider community. Leprosy damages nerves, causing a loss of feeling that can lead to physical injury. Similarly, mental and emotional trauma can cause us to lose empathy and emotional connection with others. Leprosy also affects the respiratory tract, skin, and eyes, representing an external ugliness that mirrors the inner damage caused by unresolved pain. After repeated hurt, we can become emotionally numb, losing feelings for ourselves and others, which is a sign of dying inside.

Five Faith Steps Toward Holistic Healing

Elizabeth Kubler-Ross, in her book <u>On Death and Dying,</u> describes the stages of death and dying. I have paralleled these stages as a **"Healing Process"** with the emotional/spiritual process of dying to our selfishness in a relationship, which is synonymous with discipleship for spiritual growth **(Luke 9:23-24)**. It enables us to "give" and "receive" by accepting the other person without judgment, whether we choose to be with them or not.

Just as our physical bodies have built-in immunities that fight bacteria and infectious diseases, so psychologically we have defense mechanisms that protect us from mental and emotional pain. Unfortunately, those psychological defense mechanisms can become barriers in a relationship that prevent us from receiving because of the pain of the past.

Faith Step One: Denial & Isolation

Denial is one of the defense mechanisms in our "psychology of being human" that suppresses the underlying feelings of guilt, shame, and pain. Crushing or suppressing our guilt and shame of the past does not get rid of it; it merely delays and appeases the pain. When another circumstance arises that reminds us of the past problem, the old problem is triggered, and we relive the pain and project the old problem onto the current person. We can't judge a person by our past experiences because everyone's situation is unique, and anyone can change. That's a decision you must discern based on qualities and core values.

The Psychology of Denial (Mental Justification)

When we deny the reality of our lives, it becomes a means of rationalizing and justifying wrong things that build up like sweeping dirt under the rug. Denial happens when we try to cover and appease the pain of our guilt and shame by rationalizing the past problem and excusing our responsibility.

Because the things in our past were so painful, we will bury them deep within our consciousness. When those suppressed issues are confronted in our present situations, our defenses go up to protect our emotions from pain, and we can "erupt" and walk away from dialoguing the problem. We will then put up bigger walls that deny the problem and separate ourselves from a cure. We will then lack empathy and understanding of others, which can become volatile. That's where arguing and fighting can become domestic violence.

Faith Step Two: Anger

Some of us may not be able to even talk about the past problems in our lives because of anger. Anger completely shuts the door of dialogue. The American Heritage Dictionary of the English Language defines anger as "A strong feeling of displeasure or hostility."

Bitterness is unresolved resentment that comes out in rage and fury and can become hatred if left unresolved. The Book of Hebrews warns Christians with the sad example of Esau, not to allow the problems of life to cause bitterness. *"Exercise foresight and be on the watch to look [after one another], to see that no one falls back from and fails to secure God's grace (His unmerited favor and spiritual blessing), in order that no root of resentment (rancor, bitterness, or hatred) shoots forth and causes trouble and bitter torment, and the many become contaminated and defiled by it—That no one may become guilty of sexual vice, or become a profane (godless and sacrilegious) person as Esau did, who sold his own birthright for a single meal"* **(Hebrews 12:15-16)**.

The word bitter there comes from a root word for bile. Bile becomes poisonous when it stays in the gallbladder too long. If we store up anger and resentful feelings for too long, causing bitterness, like bile stored too long in the gallbladder, it can secrete poison into our psychological and emotional system, causing us to feel sick. Anger is a normal human emotion, but anger ceases to be normal when it becomes bitter. *"When angry, do not sin; do not ever let your wrath (your exasperation, your fury or indignation) last until the sun goes down. Leave no [such] room or foothold for the devil [give no opportunity to him]"* **(Ephesians 4:26-27)**. Learn to repent and forgive daily.

The Psychology of Anger (Pointing Fingers)

Blame can be defined as the projection of one's faults onto others. Christ talked about judging others in **Matthew 7:1-5,** like projecting personal subjective faults onto others. In other words, when we are judgmental of others, it's like punishing ourselves by putting them down for the sake of lifting ourselves.

A believer or any person, for that matter, responsibility is not about blame, it's about assuming some responsibility in our lives for existing problems, either because of what we did or didn't do—omission and commission. A good analogy for this is about kids growing up in the same household. Sometimes parents can see trash next to one of their kids in the house and will say, "Please pick it up." Most kids would respond by saying, "I didn't drop it." Then the parent could say, "I'm not accusing you of dropping it. I'm asking you to assume some responsibility and pick it up." To move on in the healing process, we must assume some responsibility for problems in our lives without "blaming" ourselves or others. Life is filled with problems that come uninvited, as we see in the Book of Job.

Our responsibility is not "direct," but "indirect," meaning our lack of responsibility may not be because of what we did but maybe because of what we did not do. Assuming responsibility puts the issue in perspective to understand the origin of the anger. Why Am I So Angry!?

Faith Step Three: Bargaining

Bargaining begins where anger ends. When we can no longer "label" and "stereotype" other people as wrong and bad people, we will become angry. *"When a man is wrong and refuses to admit it, he will always get angry"* —**Haliburten**. We become angry because we have been wrong about people, and bargaining takes the place of anger, especially when we can no longer justify our wrong feelings and opinions.

The truth is that we cannot bargain with God to change His Word, and His Word commands that we resolve our problems and reconcile with people when we can **(II Corinthians 5:16-21)**. When we can no longer have our way, we begin to lose control of those prejudiced opinions and feelings that have fed into our dislike of people.

In the world of business, bargaining is the exchange of goods and services at a lower than market price. Bargaining gets something cheaper than standard to make a profit for the bargainer. There is no cheap way to achieve the resolution of our problems without paying the required price. There are no *"cutting" corners*.

The Psychology of Bargaining (Postponing the Inevitable)

Bargaining begins by taking the wrong approach to a problem. Bargaining here is bartering with God and us by exchanging our anger and conviction for something easier that doesn't require involvement or commitment. We try to do something good, unassociated with the problem, to feel better about ourselves, to outweigh the bad, which only delays the problem. Doing good can be good only if it doesn't exclude those whom we think are the perpetrators of the problem. Moving on and getting over an issue doesn't mean we ignore the necessary steps to forgive from the heart.

Faith Step Four: Depression

Depression happens when we run out of the wrong things to do as we try to bargain with God.

Depression occurs when we run into the only right thing to do: Confess, Repent, Forgive, and Restore. We become sad because we have been wrong about people for so long.

The Psychology of Depression (Giving up Control)

When we come to grips with our responsibility to resolve and reconcile our problems with people, we are at the point of forfeiting former controls and wrong opinions of people. Stereotypes and labels come off, and we are ready to accept the fact that they are just different, wrong, or right, then we can move on. In this stage of depression, we are actually dying to our "selfishness" and becoming true disciples of the Lord—Bearing Our Cross.

Giving up control feels like a loss. The losses that we feel at this stage can be many-faceted. It can be from the loss of control that we once exercised over others. It can also come from the sacrifice of status and the time that it will take to reconcile. It is a worthy "sacrifice" that will gain God's approval and rewards down the road. The greatest reward will be "freedom" and "deliverance" from toxic thoughts and feelings that make us feel sick. *"My sacrifice [the sacrifice acceptable] to God is a broken spirit; a broken and a contrite heart [broken down with sorrow for sin and humbly and thoroughly penitent], such, O God, You will not despise"* **(Psalms 51:17).**

Faith Step Five: Acceptance

Acceptance is the final stage of surrender. It is the stage where we cease from our struggles about resolving and reconciling our problems as the Will of God. It brings us into the place of Christ's Lordship, and the influences of society, family, or friends no longer intimidate us to avoid our problems. It is the phase in the process of healing where we have come out of denial. We have also released our anger and ceased bargaining with God. Now we have overcome depression and are ready to accept the differences between people.

The Psychology of Acceptance (Embraced Differences)

Acceptance here means to receive someone favorably with approval. Not only should we refuse to hold the differences of people against them, but believers should embrace their "neutral" differences with value and appreciation. Approval does not mean that God condones the error of our ways, but tolerates our weaknesses and human frailties associated with the error of our ways. Within relationships, approval implies support.

Frequently, people struggle to understand the differences in their respective *cultural* and *life experiences*. Their effort usually fails because of the cultural-experience dilemma that exists between them. Due to very different experiences, we will never be able to accept each other if we try to understand each other first. We must realize that acceptance precedes understanding.

Acceptance will initiate the process of getting to know and understand each other. When we accept each other with all our differences intact, it allows for the beginning of a relationship. Understanding says, "I will not have a relationship with you until I can understand you first." Acceptance says, "I will accept you and then get to know you, then understand you."

For a believer, acceptance grows out of their relationship with the Lord. The Lord accepts all believers on the merits of His love, and His blood "blots out" our erroneous differences. When we receive Christ, we enter a growing, loving relationship with the Lord. Every day we learn more about the Lord. An understanding relationship begins with acceptance.

Acceptance ends by putting a period on the things that were discussed, including the differences in views on the problem or issues. My 95-year-old mother-in-law lays out the wisdom for acceptance in her cliché words, "Open the window and shut the door." In practical application to accept those words means airing the problems out (open the window) and not letting them back in (shut the door).

Faith & Works Make it Happen

We cannot magically and mystically make the reality of what we believe to happen. That's called metaphysics, a form of parapsychology, essentially witchcraft used wittingly and unwittingly by those who have opted for a positive confession form of faith developed by men. That form of erroneous faith leads adherents from a focus on the Lord to focus on "faith in faith," which will "shipwreck" their faith in the Lord **(1 Timothy 1:18-20)**.

Those who have participated in movements in the church that have displaced "saving faith" to a "prosperity gospel" by misinterpreting and misaligning fundamental Scripture like **Proverbs 23:7** do not mean you will have what you envision in your mind and put on a vision board and confess into reality. The text means, relative to the King's words to a young man, that your thoughts are precipitators to action. In other words, you will do what's in your mind if you think about it long enough. Then there is the misinterpretation of **Hebrews 11:3**.

Although there is nothing impossible with God, biblical faith is believing in the possible and then working towards it.

When it comes to salvation, the Apostle Paul speaks of faith without works as the favor of the work of grace by the Lord on the Cross. James speaks of salvation coupled with works as proof of salvation. There isn't a contradiction between the two views. **THE POINT IS, WHATEVER WE BELIEVE, WE WILL WORK TOWARDS ACHIEVING IT BY DOING WHAT'S IN OUR MINDS AND HEARTS.** In that context, the beginning of faith that delivers is desiring spiritual growth in our lives first and foremost, which is synonymous with seeking the Kingdom of God first, and everything else that we need and desire will be added. So, we can believe in healing in our spirit, soul, and body, but healing in that context is a process. We can believe and experience the restoration of broken relationships, financial increases, etc. But if we believe those things, we will work toward them.

Healing is a progressive process, like the lepers who were healed as they went. In **Luke 17:11-17**, there was a situation where the Lord was traveling between the border towns of Samaria and Galilee and encountered twelve lepers who yelled at him from a distance, asking for "mercy," or to be healed. The Lord immediately responded by fast-forwarding them to go see a professional by saying, *"Go, show yourselves to the priest."* That was the custom to verify and confirm that they were healed, and they were **"cleansed"** of their dreaded disease as they went along the way.

But only one leper thanked the Lord. He was a foreigner; more than likely, the hated, despised, racially and religiously mixed Samaritans. Then the Lord said, *"Rise and go; your faith has made you well."* That's where healing begins, our faith. Real biblical saving faith is about taking God at His Word and believing over time, no matter how long it takes for needed change to come.

My Brokenness as a Wounded Healer

The Dynamics of Change

Change is an inevitable part of life, manifesting in both positive and negative ways. Just as transformation occurs within the plant and animal kingdoms through various conditions, so too does change shape humanity. People, circumstances, trials, tribulations, and temptations are all forces that mold us into who we are, shaped by God's Word and Spirit.

Reflecting on my own journey, I recognize that I am not the same person I once was—I am better, renewed through experiences and growth. And so it should be with every disciple of Christ—getting better and better—going from *faith* to *faith*, *grace* to *grace*, *strength* to *strength*, and *glory* to *glory*.

The Potter's House Reflection

Jeremiah 18:1-6 tells the story of the Potter's House, where the prophet witnesses flawed clay being remolded into a new vessel. This metaphor illustrates how, as believers, our lives may become misshapen through painful events. God, acting as the Potter, removes our flaws and reshapes us in His image, making us whole. Like clay being molded, the process of transformation is often uncomfortable, involving being mashed, flattened, and squeezed, yet it is through these trials that renewal occurs. My own journey saw me out of shape for five years, and then, over the next five years, I gradually became a new version of myself—though the transformation was not yet complete. Healing from prostate cancer marked a significant turning point, drawing me closer to the Lord than ever before. Sickness and near-death experiences can awaken us to deeper truths.

Prostate Cancer Diagnosis: Facing a Critical Decision

In 2019, I was diagnosed with prostate cancer. My urologist offered several treatment options, including chemotherapy, but I chose to decline all except for the surgical removal of my prostate. Despite the risk of erectile dysfunction—a common concern for men—I made this choice anchored in my faith in Jesus Christ, the Great Physician. Three months before my diagnosis in September 2019, I sensed the Lord's voice during meditation, assuring me, "You will encounter cancer, but it will be like a hiccup and a bump in the road." This reassurance allowed me to trust that healing would come through the hands of medical professionals.

Surgery, Recovery, and New Beginnings

With confidence and assurance, I underwent surgery in December 2019. Surrounded by my family, I approached the procedure with a positive outlook, believing I would emerge cancer-free. Upon waking, my wife was by my side, and the next day, I was walking around the hospital ward. Soon after, I was discharged and, within three days at home, able to jog lightly indoors. Since then, I have maintained a moderate exercise routine and have remained cancer-free for seven years.

Encouragement for Others Facing Adversity

By sharing my journey, I hope to encourage other men facing similar life-threatening conditions. It is important not to fear living—even in the shadow of illness. Personally, I am unafraid of death, confident in my eternal destination and the promise of new life. My message is this: although Christ paid the debt for our sins, we still experience the consequences of our actions. As believers, it is essential to confront our circumstances with grace and dignity, maintaining confidence and integrity throughout our trials.

Facing Trouble with Positive Reflections

Aside from the affair previously discussed and other mistakes detailed in this book, I faced each challenge head-on, holding my head high, not in arrogance, but with dignity in knowing that I wasn't the type of man that others judged me as. Today, I live with a clean slate—my past wrongs washed away by God's forgiveness. I am blessed with a healthy, intimate relationship with my wife, as seen in the poetic, metaphoric words of Solomon in the Song of Solomon, and the hope of heaven ahead.

My New Role in Ministry

My ministry as a Wounded Healer—specifically as a Mission Developer—centers on fostering unity among Afrocentric people and preparing them for reconciliation with all people. The task of unifying Afrocentric communities is complex and challenging, yet possible. Below, I examine the difficulties and the opportunities for greater unity.

—Historical Barriers to Unity—

The struggle to unite Afrocentric people is deeply rooted in historical circumstances. During the Jim Crow era in the South, racial segregation was legally enforced ("De Jure"), while in the North, it existed as a social reality ("De Facto"). Afrocentric individuals were relegated to neighborhoods separated from mainstream society. The Supreme

Court's 1896 "separate but equal" decision led to widespread discrimination, with Afrocentric Americans living in and around the poorest communities and facing restricted housing opportunities. However, after the Supreme Court overturned these policies with Brown v. Board of Education in 1954, and the Civil Rights Act of 1964 promoted integration, affluent Afrocentric Americans began moving to suburban neighborhoods, forming a middle class. This migration resulted in middle-class Afrocentric Americans adopting dominant cultural norms. Sociologists termed the departure of Eurocentric Americans from these neighborhoods as "white flight," while the departure of Afrocentric Americans was called "brown flight." Psychologists, referencing Kenneth and Mamie Clark's "doll test," which showed black children preferred the white doll over the black doll, suggested that such movement fostered a "self-hate psychology," with preferences for Eurocentric symbols and culture, and slang terms towards those who left as "Bougie" or "Bougee," highlighting internal divisions.

Social and Economic Divisions

A major barrier to unity is the gap between the "Haves and Have Nots." Wealth disparities and materialism divide Afrocentric communities. Attempts to combat problems associated with poverty with achievement and prosperity through their Judeo/Christian values serve as a wedge between them. The negative rhetoric usually comes from traditional church members who criticize low-income communities, further driving them away from the church. Sometimes, extreme attitudes of superiority within the community exacerbate separation by combating bigotry with bigotry, which appears as siding with the Eurocentric culture.

Faith-Based Divisions

Faith also contributes to division among Afrocentric people in two significant ways. First, denominational and non-denominational churches maintain sharp theological and doctrinal boundaries, limiting collaboration and association. Traditional Afrocentric churches have a residue of historical elements of the historical Eurocentric church that usually conflict with non-denominational churches, especially the mega church. Second, some Afrocentric movements outside of Christianity distance themselves from traditional Christianity, viewing it as a Eurocentric institution that deifies Eurocentric Christianity as racially superior to Afrocentric people. This distinction is based on Afrocentric people's mutual faith differences being rejected, resulting in rejection of each other. This mutual exclusivity prevents unity and discourages traditional Afrocentric Christian leaders from challenging societal power structures or supporting others within the community because they see it as a socialist movement separated from the gospel.

Political and Social Divisions

Political affiliations and social perspectives further fragment Afrocentric communities. Divergent party allegiances shape differing views on American identity and priorities for the community, creating additional separation.

Bi-Racial Relationships and Their Impact on Unity

Bi-racial relationships and marriages can sometimes pose barriers within Afrocentric communities as one within the relationship aligns more with the other's culture. Usually, within bi-racial relationships, the Afrocentric partner aligns more with the Eurocentric partner, resulting in distance from their culture. On the other hand, the Eurocentric partner who aligns more with the Afrocentric partner may be ostracized from their culture. Both are then put in a place of neutrality or compromise. The key is changing the narrative and conversation about multiethnic relationships by removing race from the equation. These dynamics can hinder unity within Afrocentric communities. Cultural conformity can have an effect on disparity.

A potential solution is to shift the focus from bi-racial marriages to multiethnic marriages, encouraging both partners to embrace and celebrate their cultural differences. By honoring each tradition equally, couples can create relationships that foster unity within the broader community.

Biblical Perspective on Multiethnic Cross-Cultural Relationships & Modern-Day Deliverers

God honors multiethnic cross-cultural relationships by dismantling racial barriers. Previously, I shared the migrations of Shem, Ham, and Japheth to point out that prior to their migrations and developing distinct cultures, one culture of people existed among diverse ethnicities, and co-existing among each other was the norm. I believe that is the Creator's design for relationships that accept, embrace, and celebrate their differences when they view themselves as ethnic families among the broad family of God. The Bible offers a perspective on race in relationships, as seen in **Numbers 12:1-15**, that demonstrates God's dissatisfaction with opposing multiethnic relationships. Miriam criticized Moses for marrying an African Cushite woman, revealing underlying racial prejudice. God responded by punishing Miriam with leprosy, demonstrating divine disapproval of racial discrimination in relationships.

Spiritual Perspective and Hope for Unity

Despite existing obstacles, there is hope for unity in what Scripture calls the "last days." Divisions that seem insurmountable will be overcome through divine intervention. God will raise Deliverers—anointed individuals who will unify People of Color, similar to the 144,000 mentioned in **Revelation 7:4-8** and **14:1-5**, by evangelizing and discipling God's harvest.

History provides examples of Deliverers: Freedom Fighters and Abolitionists such as Frederick Douglass, Harriet Tubman, Sojourner Truth, and John Brown, who secured freedom for many. Civil rights leaders like Martin Luther King Jr., Rosa Parks, John Lewis, Malcolm X, and Thurgood Marshall helped dismantle Jim Crow laws to bring about social justice. We can never forget that

Caucasian men and women were also a force to secure these rights.

Through faith and action, these individuals ushered in civil rights advancements for all people. Church reformers who liberated believers from religious oppression also serve as Deliverers, such as Martin Luther, much like those in the Book of Judges who rescued Israel from its enemies. These examples show how the few, empowered by God, can deliver the many.

The Role of Modern-Day Deliverers— Combating Spiritual Evil

The theme of this book has highlighted spiritual influences that affect life on the earth and how marginalized people are oppressed from a higher spiritual plane to handicap and hinder reaping God's harvest. In the real world, we see this battle in politics, religion, and social movements. But as disciples of the Lord and believers in the truth of the sacred text of Scripture, we will acknowledge that what's happened in our world is higher than the entities named. It is a battle from eternity through time between good and evil spiritual forces to control the earth and its people. Evil seeks to prevent God's Kingdom (The New Jerusalem) from coming to fruition, and good is destined to win. However, this battle involves God's Covenant People, known as the Church, but in reality, it is the Body of Christ, composed of disciples of the Lord coming together to bring to pass God's Kingdom in time, before the Lord returns.

Understanding Spiritual Battles on the Internet

On page 127, reference was made to a spiritual battle on the internet through an article entitled "The Shift." Building on that teaching, this closing section offers practical guidance for those pursuing human rights and social justice within the context of spiritual warfare.

Responding to Oppression: Overcoming Evil with Good

The phrase "fight fire with fire" is often used by individuals and organizations in response to oppression, suggesting retaliation in kind, or "doing evil for evil." This approach, however, contradicts the Kingdom Concept found in Scripture, which commands believers to "overcome evil with good" rather than repay evil with evil. It is important to recognize that this principle is intended specifically for the Community of Faith, not for political arenas.

Spiritual Protection for Advocates

The Community of Faith plays a vital role in building spiritual walls of protection around those who seek human rights and social justice, regardless of their affiliations. This protection is established through three main practices:

1. Intercessory Prayer from II Chronicles 7:14.
2. Inviting the Lord into the Affairs of life that oppress Humanity, as we see in Acts 12:1-18.

3. Active engagement in spiritual warfare, as outlined in Ephesians 6:1-18.

Practical Application: Countering Oppression

"Fighting fire with fire" is achievable in the natural world. In the natural world, firefighters use a strategy called "backburning" or "counter-firing," where they set controlled fires ahead of a wildfire to eliminate fuel and halt its advance, eventually putting out the fire. Similarly, and analogously, advocates for human rights and social justice are like firefighters. They must discern and anticipate through researched data where the injustice is going within the public and move ahead of it with countermeasures in front of it to cut it off.

This approach involves discerning the strategies of opposition—akin to playing chess, where each move is carefully considered. Believers use the "gift of discerning of spirits" to recognize and address these strategies. By identifying the opposition's next move and preparing a counter plan ahead of time, two significant outcomes are achieved:

1. The public is alerted to what is about to happen.
2. When the anticipated event occurs, the public realizes the accuracy of the prediction, leading to greater support and alignment with the cause.

As more people rally around the cause, the collective voice for truth becomes stronger. Notably, this approach does not involve protesting, marching, or interfering with law enforcement; instead, it invites God to intervene and defeat the spiritual forces behind hate and violence as it builds walls of protection around advocates and activists for justice and righteousness.

—This End Is The Beginning—

www.ingramcontent.com/pod-product-compliance
Lightning Source LLC
Chambersburg PA
CBHW061735070526
44585CB00024B/2678